NO FLOWERS . . . JUST LOTS OF JOY

No Flowers...
Just Lots of Joy

SPECIAL EDITION

FIONA CASTLE
with Jan Greenough

KINGSWAY PUBLICATIONS
EASTBOURNE

ISBN 1 84291 102 3

Published by
KINGSWAY COMMUNICATIONS LTD
Lottbridge Drove, Eastbourne BN23 6NT, England.
Email: books@kingsway.co.uk

Book design and production for the publishers by
Bookprint Creative Services, P.O. Box 827, BN21 3YJ, England.
Printed in Great Britain.

Contents

Preface to Special Edition

It has been said that you have to live life forwards, but you can only understand it backwards. That's why I'm glad to have the opportunity to write in this new edition of my book *No Flowers – Just Lots of Joy*.

This edition includes a great deal of the story I first told in *Give Us This Day* – about my early life, my marriage to Roy, how I discovered Jesus as my Saviour, and the difference it made to our marriage and my life. It also tells the story of Roy's cancer, which continued in the first edition of *No Flowers* to his death and my experience of bereavement.

Now I am happy to be able to combine those two books together with an update, and to say that today, life is good. The faithful God who sustained me through all those events is still my Saviour and my loving Father. I have been honest about my struggles and my mistakes, and I think the reality of those dark times is described well in the Graham Kendrick song I have chosen to place at the start of the first chapter. That song also summarises what I truly believe about the hardest times in our lives: 'For this I have Jesus'.

The message I hope this book brings is that our God is a loving God, who can lighten our darkness and pour his joy and hope into our hearts.

Fiona Castle

For the joys and for the sorrows,
The best and worst of times;
For this moment, for tomorrow,
For all that lies behind.
Fears that crowd around me;
For the failure of my plans;
For the dreams of all I hope to be,
The truth of what I am –

For the tears that flow in secret
In the broken times;
For the moments of elation,
Or the troubled mind;
For all the disappointments
Or the sting of old regrets;
All my prayers and longings
That seem unanswered yet –

For the weakness of my body,
The burdens of each day;
For the nights of doubt and worry
When sleep has fled away;
Needing reassurance
And the will to start again,
A steely-eyed endurance,
The strength to fight and win –

For this I have Jesus,
For this I have Jesus,
For this I have Jesus,
I have Jesus.

Graham Kendrick

8

1

God in the Background

It was the Easter of 1995 and I was at Spring Harvest – the great Christian holiday festival of teaching and praise – as a speaker. Exactly two years before I had been at the same meeting with my husband Roy, thanking the crowds of Christians there for all their support and the loving messages they had sent during his illness. That year I was there alone, because in September 1994 Roy died from lung cancer.

I was aware of the atmosphere of excitement and anticipation all around me as I made my way to the platform to join the other speakers, ready for the main evening meeting to begin. I looked out over the marquee full of over six thousand people, and my mouth went dry. I had been asked to lead them in a short prayer, and I was terrified! I am quite happy to talk about my faith to any size of group for any length of time, but I didn't feel that I could pray in front of such a huge crowd for a single minute. And I was sitting with such well-known Christians – Roger and Faith Forster were there, and Steve

Gaukroger, Luis Palau and Graham Kendrick. I felt very small and inadequate. 'Lord, help me,' I prayed silently. 'Give me your words.'

As I prayed, Graham Kendrick began to sing a new song which he had just written, and the words reached me through the waves of my panic: 'For this I have Jesus'. Roger Forster leaned over and tapped me on the arm.

'Did you hear how Graham came to write this, Fiona?' he asked. 'Charles Price was preaching and told the story of an elderly friend of his who always said "For this I have Jesus" – it was his catchphrase, and he used it on every occasion, and for everything that happened to him, good or bad! Graham heard it and it inspired him to write this song.'

As the chorus swelled around me, and six thousand voices joined in the words, I knew how I should pray, and my nervousness drained away. I got to my feet.

'I don't know all of you people here tonight,' I began, 'but Jesus does. He knows you by name, and he knows all the joys and sorrows, and all the circumstances of your life. I don't know how you have come here tonight, or what your burdens are, but I do know that whatever we are carrying, we can lay it before Jesus in perfect confidence. This is why he came – to let us know that we have a loving Father in heaven who cares for us. "He was despised and rejected by men, a man of sorrows and familiar with suffering." He understands all our feelings, so we can turn to him in trust. "For this we have Jesus." '

The prayer I prayed after that was short, but it was heartfelt, because that was the lesson that God had been teaching me all my life, and especially through all the weary months of Roy's illness; and now after his death I was still proving it to be true.

I was born in West Kirby, a small seaside town in The Wirral, in 1940. My father was a hard-working local GP, one of 'the old school' – always polite, long-suffering, and like many doctors at that time, on duty twenty-four hours a day. If he ever wanted a day off, he had to go out of town, or else he would surely be called out to visit someone. He was loved and respected by his family, patients and friends for his compassion, common sense and self-discipline – qualities he instilled in his children, too.

My mother was trained as a teacher of PE and ballroom dancing, but gave up her career when she married. But that certainly didn't mean that she stopped working! As well as running the house and caring for us she acted as secretary and receptionist for my father, often giving up a lot of time to comfort worried parents and relatives of patients, and visiting the sick and bereaved. She also cleaned three surgeries every day before breakfast.

Ours was a busy household; as well as her own four children, Mum also found herself looking after an extended family of various servicemen (Poles, Canadians and Australians) during and after the war. She darned their socks, listened to their life stories, and found ways to help them contact their own families; all while giving practical support to my father's work.

All this seemed perfectly normal to me, born during the war. I had never known anything but rationing, and I grew up in a house where there was always something going on! My brother Tony was twelve years old when I was born; he joined the Navy before the end of the war, and later became an engineer, working his way up from the shop floor in a factory in Birkenhead. My sister Liza was eleven; she later went to Art School in Liverpool and became a dress designer for Horrocks. Mauny (Maureen) was ten; she later became a secretary. So by the time I was nine, Mauny was the only other child of the family still living at home, because she was working locally.

I was happily going to the local primary school, where my favourite activity was ballet, taught by Betty Hassell of the Hammond School of Dancing. She decided that I had talent which could be fostered only by attendance at a full-time dancing school, and told my mother so. They considered various options, and finally decided on Elmhurst in Surrey – two hundred miles away! So in the summer term of 1949, when I was nine and a half years old, I was dressed in my grey and blue uniform, and went off to boarding school for the first time.

The routine at Elmhurst was incredibly disciplined; as well as our academic work and our dance classes, we were also expected to sweep the studios, serve at tables and wash up after meals. As food was still rationed the meals were very basic, and we were always hungry. At tea there was bread with a thin scrape of jam (no butter). When we were responsible for preparing the food we would spread some slices more thickly and hide them on the piled plate, where we knew we could retrieve them later!

I was happy enough for the first year, but succumbed to a wave of dreadful homesickness at the beginning of the second. I wrote pathetic letters home to my mother, which she ignored, sending me brief and cheerful replies which never referred to my complaints. Eventually I realised that nothing was going to come of my pleadings, so I might as well settle down and get on with life. It was a good example of my mother's firm belief in self-discipline and common sense: she forced us to make our own way and stick to the course we were committed to. A similar struggle took place over the academic work: some students were enjoying five or six hours dancing a day, with the minimum of lessons. My parents decided that I must make an attempt at O levels, which restricted my dancing to one class a day, with the rest of the time being spent studying. In retrospect I appreciate their insistence; though I was never destined to be brilliant academically, it was another lesson in sticking to a task whether or not I was enjoying it, and learning the discipline of working towards a goal.

After O levels I returned to school to concentrate entirely on what the school taught best: dance, drama and stagecraft. Oh, the joy and freedom of being allowed to dance after all; to work towards the career in show business I longed for. I had a very happy time, especially at the end of the autumn term when I was released from school for four weeks to join a repertory company in pantomime at Worthing. I spent the following summer in the chorus at the Pavilion Theatre in Bournemouth, and finally left school that winter, when I danced in the chorus for *Puss in Boots* at the Coventry Hippodrome.

At last I was tasting real freedom – earning my own living by doing the thing I loved to do most of all; the best kind of independence. I hadn't been let loose on the world entirely alone, however: the chaplain of Elmhurst School had arranged lodgings for three of us with a married couple who were friends of his, so we were fairly strictly chaperoned, much to my parents' relief. In fact, the world of show business which I was entering was by no means the wild and unstructured lifestyle that perhaps they had feared. Quite apart from the supportive hand of the school chaplain as I started out, my outlook was still very much governed by my religion.

As a child I was taken to church every Sunday, though I sometimes think the most useful thing I learned was how to sit still for an hour. The emphasis of the teaching was that Jesus was a 'pattern' for us, and I can still recall deciding that I would have to try to be as good as Jesus. My resolve lasted one day – even in my innocent childish world the going was too tough – and I realised that I couldn't manage to be entirely good purely by my own devices. At Elmhurst the religious life was very strong, and the beautiful chapel played a central role in our lives. The flavour was 'high' Church of England, with all the ritual that implies. Night and morning a prayer bell sounded, when we were supposed to stop whatever we were doing and drop to our knees for prayer until a second bell released us, about three minutes later. There was a daily morning service in chapel, communion three times a week, and on Sundays we went to both morning and evening services. Understandably, one of my goals was to be confirmed and take a full part in the church's life, and so I was prepared and confirmed when I was twelve. I took this as seriously as I could, within the limits of my understanding, but I had no real concept of the mysterious Holy Spirit. Most of my understanding of Christianity centred around the ceremonies of the church services, rather than the everyday reality of knowing Jesus as a Saviour and friend. In some ways this hampered me throughout the subsequent years, as I went on dutifully seeking God through attendance at church and my own efforts to be 'good enough'.

Because church was so important to me, I always made great efforts to attend on Sundays, wherever I happened to be working – unless I was touring, in which case most of Sunday always seemed to be taken up with standing on Crewe station! I realise now how powerful are the standards we set our children: because my parents and my school had both insisted on the importance of attendance at church, I struggled dutifully with a discipline I imposed upon myself, and suffered dreadful guilt if I failed. My parents certainly pointed me in the right direction spiritually and morally, and as I was not by nature a rebellious person, I did my best to follow their example. But in the matter of faith we each have to discover the reality for ourselves, and a 'handed-down' faith will not work. I'm afraid it took me a long time, with many heartaches along the way, to discover the living reality for myself.

Once I had left school and was 'resting' between shows, I went back to live with my parents: by this time my father had retired from general practice and they had moved to a cottage in the Chilterns. Being ambitious, I decided I needed to do more than dance in the chorus, so that autumn I came to a momentous decision. I would give myself a time-limit – say, until the next Christmas season – and if I couldn't manage to secure a decent part for myself in a Christmas production, I would give up show business and do something sensible!

Fortunately for me, a series of opportunities made that Christmas a very special one. To begin with, the Royal Shakespeare Company had arranged their first-ever tour in Russia. This left the Royal Shakespeare Theatre in Stratford-upon-Avon empty, and unbelievably, someone decided to stage *Mother Goose* in it. I don't believe that such a production had ever taken place there before (or since). Certainly Billy Dainty and Ethel Revenal had never performed there before – and I had managed to get the part of Principal Girl!

That role led to others, and I began to feel more established. I left home and set up in a flat in London with an old school friend, Louanne Richards, who was working with the Royal Ballet Company. A year or so later I auditioned for the part of Liesl in *The Sound of Music*: the part was given to Barbara Brown, but I accepted the alternative of being her understudy. I stayed for two years, eventually taking over the part of Liesl when Barbara left to have a baby, and before that filling in as one of the nuns or in other small parts.

It was a good feeling to be part of such a big production, and especially to be no longer at the mercy of the short runs of pantomime and summer seasons. To be employed for two years continuously is something of a dancer's dream! But I suppose I did miss the constant change of venue, and the new faces each year. Over my time in variety shows I had made many good friends, such as Harry Secombe and Eric Morecambe and his wife and family. One evening I was watching TV with the Morecambes when Roy Castle appeared on the screen. I'd seen Roy at the London Palladium shortly after his success at the Royal Variety Performance, and thought he was a brilliant entertainer.

'Have you ever worked with Roy Castle, Eric?' I asked casually.

'Once or twice,' replied Eric. 'Good, isn't he?'

'Mmm. If you get the chance, would you introduce me?'

'Course I will,' said Eric, and nothing more was said. I assumed that he would forget all about it, but about a year later I got a phone call from Eric, saying that he was doing a TV show at the Wood Green Empire with Roy, and suggesting that I went to the show with his wife, Joan.

I was looking forward to the show until Eric dropped a bombshell. He took me round to Roy's dressing room and put his head round the door.

'Roy,' he said, 'this is Fiona and she's in love with you,' and promptly left! I could cheerfully have strangled Eric, who didn't care in the least that he had left me blushing and desperately embarrassed, trying to gather my wits to start a conversation.

As it happened, Roy was as shy as I was, and when we went out after the show for a meal with Eric and Ernie, Joan, Dickie Valentine and the whole of Chris Barber's Jazz Band, we didn't do very much talking. I must admit that I spent the next few days in a state of great expectation, hoping that Roy would ring or write, but nothing came. I resigned myself to the fact that the great romance I'd been imagining just wasn't going to happen. However, Eric, apart from being a very staunch friend, was not a man to give up easily. Morecambe and Wise were working at The London Palladium for the season with Roy, and Eric overheard Ernie Wise and his wife Doreen invite Roy out to dinner – 'with your girlfriend, of course.'

Roy looked embarrassed. 'Er – I haven't got a girlfriend,' he confessed.

Eric was delighted. 'No trouble, ' he said. 'We'll fix you up in no time.' He picked up the phone and dialled my number at the theatre. 'Fiona, get round here right away,' he ordered. 'Roy's taking you out!'

The girls in the show came to my aid. I was wearing jeans and a tatty sweater, being prepared for nothing after the performance other than going home and putting my feet up. Five minutes later I was made up, dressed in borrowed clothes, and setting off like Cinderella to the ball, leaving the others to trail home in my scruffy outfit.

We had a lovely meal in a smart restaurant – a rare treat for me – and afterwards Roy plucked up sufficient courage to ask me out himself. We seemed to be on the same wavelength from the start, though Roy later teased me about some early doubts he had.

'We went back to the flat for coffee,' he recalled, 'and when you opened the fridge door to get the milk out, I could see that there was nothing at all inside except a tiny cube of cheese. And I thought, "Oh, dear, we'll be eating out of tins with this one!"'

In spite of his doubts about my housekeeping abilities,

it really was the beginning of a wonderful relationship. At first I could hardly believe it was happening to me. Roy was quite a big star, both on TV and on the show circuit, while I was completely unknown. I found it a very strange sensation when I first saw our picture in the newspapers, as I wasn't used to publicity, but Roy took it all in his stride.

'You'll get used to it,' was all he said. 'Especially once we're married.'

Roy and I were married on a gloriously sunny day in July 1963. Harry Secombe was our best man, and although Eric Morecambe was unable to be there, he was represented by his small daughter Gail, who was one of my bridesmaids. It was a big wedding, organised with much care and love by my parents, who were rather bemused at finding themselves with such a famous son-in-law. However, I think they may have been secretly relieved that at last I was doing something as normal as getting married: I had decided to leave *The Sound of Music* so that I would be free to travel with Roy. I didn't plan to join him on the stage or have anything to do with his work – Roy had seen other entertainers who had trouble with their wives interfering in their business, disagreeing with agents and so on. So I was just going to be an ordinary wife. In effect, I was giving up my career in show business to devote myself to him.

After the wedding, we sailed off across the Atlantic to spend our honeymoon in New York and Bermuda – both places where Roy was to be working, but none the less exotic and luxurious for that, especially to me, who had always lived a relatively modest lifestyle on a very limited income. Roy was more used to it by then, but he too had spent a lot of time working his way up through the clubs and cabarets and summer seasons, so he enjoyed everything doubly – partly for its own sake, and partly through my astonished amazement at our cabin on the ship, the luxury of our hotel rooms, and the welcome we received everywhere we went.

The whole of the first two years of our marriage passed in a rush. We crossed and recrossed the Atlantic as Roy had bookings in England as well as TV shows in America, and the full, busy life we led scarcely gave me a moment to reflect on the career I had given up, or to consider whether I missed the theatre. Our life wasn't all luxury hotels: sometimes we were staying in grubby digs with damp beds and unwashed linen! To begin with we didn't have a base in England, and stayed with one or other set of parents between shows. However, eventually Roy's parents moved to a smaller house by the sea, and we took over their old house in Surrey.

Two years after we married, our first baby, Daniel, was born. Roy was about to set off on the American tour of *Pickwick*, with Harry Secombe, so Daniel was christened when he was only eight days old, so that Roy could be there. Two days later Roy set off to join the rest of the company, literally leaving me holding the baby. As soon as I'd had my post-natal check at six weeks, we flew to Detroit to join him. This sounds like an amazingly confident and competent thing to do – in reality I was feeling quite the opposite. I was immensely grateful for the gentle expertise of Myra Secombe, who could calm a crying baby – and his mother – in no time. Daniel became a very well-travelled baby indeed: he spent his first birthday in Hollywood, where Roy was filming a TV special of *Alice Through the Looking Glass*.

By the time Julia was born in 1967 we had decided to look for a larger home in England; friends were surprised when we bought a six-bedroomed house in Gerrards Cross, but we told them cheerfully that we intended to fill it! I still managed to travel with Roy to many of his bookings, though it was becoming increasingly difficult: the children were often unsettled by the change of surroundings, and I was tired of constantly packing and unpacking the vast quantities of equipment they needed.

One summer we rented a little house in Bournemouth while Roy was doing a short summer season there. It was an ideal situation, close to the beach where the children could play, and with no hotel timetables or other guests to stop us doing exactly as we liked. We should have been blissfully happy, but somehow tension began to grow between us. Roy would be out all evening, but I never had a welcome for him when he got back. I was snappy and irritable, and felt tired all the time. We stopped short of major arguments, because somehow we would always come to our senses and patch up our differences just in time. However, I did realise that things were not right, and when we got home to Gerrards Cross I went to the doctor for help.

'I'm sorry to bother you,' I began. 'I just don't seem to be able to pull myself together. I feel so depressed and miserable all the time, and I'm beginning to take it out on the family. What can I do?'

The doctor was reassuring. 'More women than you realise suffer the same problems,' he said, 'but not many have the courage to own up to it.' He prescribed some medication which he said would help me to relax, and I went away feeling slightly better. At least I wasn't being entirely unreasonable, especially if my depression was something other people suffered too. In fact, I felt so encouraged that I never got round to taking the tablets, which was just as well because soon afterwards I realised that I was expecting our third baby. That doctor subsequently moved away, and I never had the courage to confess to anyone else what I was feeling – from then on I just endured it alone.

In fact, of course, I wasn't alone – Roy was enduring it with me, but as he was so often the focus of my irritability and unhappiness, I never thought about him as sharing in my misery. Over the next few years I became more and more moody and unpredictable. When Antonia was born in 1969 I decided that our travelling days were over – taking three children around with us was too daunting to contemplate. Our family was completed by Benjamin, who arrived four years later in 1973, and although he was a contented baby, the extra work-load and tiredness meant that my depression returned worse than ever.

Part of the problem was that I began to resent Roy's apparent freedom. The phone would ring with the offer of a job, and off he would go for weeks at a time. And somehow, things that worked perfectly all the time he was at home, suddenly seemed to break down as soon as he left. It seemed that no sooner had he left the house than the plumbing started leaking, the cooker stopped working, and all the children caught chicken pox! Of course I coped – I called the plumber and the repair man and got the children's prescriptions, but I felt constantly under pressure. Why wasn't Roy ever there when I needed him? The house, which had once seemed such a refuge from the pressures of travelling, socialising and the intrusions of the press, came instead to feel like a prison.

Another difficulty was that my own childhood had been very organised – there was always strict discipline, first at home and then at boarding school – so I ran my own home in the same way. It was very important to me that my house should always be clean and tidy, that the children should be beautifully dressed and well behaved, that I should cook excellent meals and that I should always look my best. My standards were much too high, and I was trapped by them. I would work all day and half the night to keep things as I thought they should be, not realising that the lovely home I thought I was making for Roy and the children was being made miserable by my obsession with perfection.

When Roy was away I kept going largely on nervous tension, not eating or sleeping properly, and of course there was an inevitable price to be paid. Roy would return, and as soon as he came through the door (probably tired from travelling, and looking forward to a loving welcome from the family he'd been missing) I would greet him with an outpouring of how awful things had been, how tired and lonely I was, and how inconsiderate he was to disturb the children when I'd just got them settled for bed! Many times, he told me afterwards, he wished he could turn round and go straight back out again.

I felt miserable, lonely and isolated; tired and yet ceaselessly energetic, as I drove myself to keep going from one task to the next. I was never hungry, so I would miss meals and then eat a handful of biscuits before bed, and wonder why I couldn't sleep. The more tired I became, the more erratic was my behaviour: I would hug the children one minute and shout at them the next, and I felt continually guilty that I wasn't being either a good mother or a good wife, yet I seemed to be powerless to break out of the pattern.

I never confided in anyone about how I was feeling, because it was very important to me that we should appear to be an idyllically happy family. I felt I had to keep up a front, the more so because Roy was well known, and I felt that much was expected of me. People assumed that life in show business was always glamorous, and whenever the press wrote about us they always spoke about 'the Castles' happy marriage'. I needed to appear to be a success, and the result was that I lived behind a mask.

This was never more apparent than when we went to church on Sundays. It was one of the things I insisted on: regular attendance at church had always been one of the fundamental rules of my childhood, and I wanted it to be the same for my children. Roy always came with us whenever he was at home, and he endured the Sunday-morning panic stoically. I would rush from bedroom to bedroom, screeching at the children, and dash to the kitchen to put the lunch in the oven.

'I don't know why you bother going to church,' Roy

said to me one morning. 'By the time you get the children organised you're in such a bad temper that it can't possibly do you any good.'

He was right, of course, because I would sink into the pew exhausted, and immediately start to think about all the jobs I still had to do when we got home, to be ready for lunch with visitors. But the minute we stepped inside the church door, the mask would be fixed in place, and the Castles would smile a peaceful Sunday smile at their tidy, well behaved children, as though everything was well in their world.

It never occurred to me that church might be a place where I could find the solution to my problem – for by now church had become part of the problem. There were times, when the depression was at its worst, when I would fantasise about curling up under the bedclothes and never emerging. Roy could see that I was becoming more and more isolated, so he suggested various activities to get me out of the house: helping with the jumble sale, driving elderly people to hospital, sitting on committees for local charities. I took it all on, and simply added to the burdens I was already carrying. All the church activities became part of the treadmill on which I drove myself, trying to succeed as a wife, a mother, a church member; coming closer and closer to exhaustion and breakdown, behind a bright and public smile. I knew that I couldn't go on much longer, but I had no idea how I could change the way I lived my life.

2
New Life

One morning I woke up under a particularly black cloud. Roy was working downstairs when I took the children to school; as soon as I got back I settled Benjamin for a nap, then went up to the bedroom, closed the door, and sank down on my knees beside the bed.

'O God,' I prayed, 'if you're there at all, you've got to help me and you've got to help me now, because I've had it. I just can't cope any longer.' I got up then – I didn't really expect an answer. I didn't know if God cared, or if he was able to do anything to help me. Almost immediately the phone began ringing, and I picked it up wearily.

It was someone I knew only slightly, and she had a very strange request.

'Fiona,' she began, 'I don't really know why I'm phoning but I had this urge to contact you. Can we meet for coffee some time? I don't really know why, or what we'll talk about when we meet, but I just have this feeling that we need to get together.'

I recalled that Tamara was a friend of my sister's – what

she called a 'committed Christian' – which in my book meant someone who had gone overboard a bit, and insisted on talking about religion all the time! In my present state I was in no mood for making dates for coffee, so I put her off.

'That would be lovely,' I lied smoothly, 'but I'm afraid I'm rather busy this week. Can we make a date for next week some time?' We consulted our diaries, made a date for the following week, and rang off.

Then I stopped and stared at the phone. A minute before I had been down on my knees, begging God for help. Here was a Christian ringing to offer me that help and I had put her off for a week! I seized the phone and tried to remember her number. I wasn't even sure of her husband's initial, and rang two or three wrong numbers before I got her again. 'Can I come round straight away, instead?' I asked. She agreed without argument.

Ben was awake now, so I picked him up, went downstairs and thrust him into Roy's arms, saying 'I'm going out' – and left. Things were so bad between us at the time that Roy thought that perhaps I really was leaving for good.

At Tamara's house I poured out all my problems, which probably didn't sound that serious to her. Rationally, I had nothing at all to be depressed about: materially I had everything I needed, I had a loving husband who provided for me and four beautiful, healthy children. What more could anyone want? It all served only to make me feel guilty about the way I was behaving. I was lonely, empty, bitter and resentful. I had everything and I had nothing. I had tried every way I knew to make life tolerable for myself and my family, and I had failed. Surely there was more to life than I had found, or what was the point in going on? If God existed and cared about us, why did he make it so hard to find him and follow him? I blurted out question after question through tears of guilt, frustration and tiredness.

Tamara listened patiently to all this and then said quietly, 'Fiona, you say that you're a Christian, that you've been going to church all your life. But have you ever actually stopped and asked Jesus to come in and take over your life?'

I was dumbfounded. 'No,' I replied, 'I didn't realise I was supposed to.' I really hadn't ever thought about it. After all, I had been christened and confirmed, went to communion regularly, and did everything I was meant to do. 'Why should I do that? Would it make any difference?'

'I think it would,' she replied gently. 'Don't you think it's about time you did it?'

'Yes, I suppose so,' I said weakly – though I think I only said it because I was afraid to say no! My back was against the wall, and I was desperate enough to try anything. Deep down I was afraid that what I was about to do would mean that I would have to try even harder, do even more, give things up and generally earn God's approval the hard way. I didn't have much faith in my ability to succeed at that. But Tamara explained to me that this wasn't about me 'doing' anything except opening my heart and letting Jesus come in. He had done the work already. By his death he had 'earned' salvation for all of us. She herself had suffered from depression for many years, so she didn't belittle my feelings and experiences, but she told me how her life had been transformed by taking this same step.

'Well,' I thought, 'at least she knows what I'm going through. If it has worked for her, maybe it will work for me.'

Tamara read me a verse from the Bible: 'Look! I have been standing at the door and I am constantly knocking. If anyone hears me calling him and opens the door, I will come in and enjoy fellowship with him and he with me' (Revelation 3:20, *Living Bible*). She closed her eyes and began to pray for me and with me. I had never prayed out loud without a prayer book before, and if I hadn't been crying so much I would have been embarrassed.

'Now, Fiona, ' she said. 'I want you to think whether there is any area of your life which is not pleasing to God. Confess it and ask for his forgiveness.' It was a solemn moment, but I wondered fleetingly if we had enough time for all the things I needed to confess! For the first time I admitted to myself and to God the mess I had made of everything that was important to me, my family, my marriage, everything.

'Lord, please forgive me,' I prayed. 'Jesus, please come into my life and make it new.'

I realised that Jesus had been standing and knocking at the door of my heart for thirty-five years; I had never let him in, and he wouldn't force the door from his side, because he had given me free will to choose what I did with my life. As soon as I prayed that prayer, he kept his promise and came into my life, and turned it upside down. I didn't become perfect, but I knew that he had come, because I did feel the most incredible sense of peace filling my heart. It was as though someone had poured warm oil all over me, touching and soothing all the sore and hurting places in my life, and all my tensions and fears and misery drained away. I knew something real and important had happened, though I didn't fully understand how. I knew that whatever happened now, I had Jesus living in me, and I would be able to cope. Life was going to be a new adventure from now on.

As I drove home that day the peace and joy I had experienced stayed with me – I even started singing in the car – and I wondered what was going to happen next. After all, I might feel the assurance that God was with me, and that I was a new person, but my circumstances were still the same. I still had the same home to run, the same family to care for and work for, the same husband with the same job. Would my feelings of peace evaporate as soon as I opened the front door?

It was only a short journey home, but during that time God showed me that I should not burst in and tell Roy what had happened. Indeed, reason told me that if I did, Roy would probably think that I'd finally flipped. My behaviour in recent weeks had been so erratic that he would have been perfectly justified in thinking that I had religious mania on top of everything, and was certifiable at last! I did notice a look of surprise and relief on his face when I went back into the house (probably because he really had been wondering if I had left him for good), but he didn't question where I had been. I realised that I had to show Roy, not just tell him what had happened – I had to let him see for himself that I really had changed. And I needed to see that for myself, too.

Roy's experience of Jesus was quite different from mine. He had been brought up to go to church regularly, and he sang in the choir in the Methodist church they attended. Church in itself he didn't find very helpful, but he seemed to grow up with a faith that grew with him. When we discussed it, much later, he put it like this:

'I always felt as though someone was holding my hand – but it was a long time before I looked up and saw whose hand I was holding.'

I had grown up surrounded by the structures of a denomination, but without the reality of a relationship with God. When at last the two came together, things began to make sense. Roy, on the other hand, had slipped out of the habit of going to church fairly early, but he had never lost the experience of daily contact with God. He followed the Master in a very simple way, praying and always trusting God to show him the right thing to do.

When he met me, he was very confused by my insistence on all the rituals of the church, when it was clear that my life did not show any sign that I knew how to listen to God as he had learned to do. Roy was always immensely patient with my emphasis on duty – even when it disrupted our family life. Now I knew that I had to show him that things really were going to be different, without making any extravagant claims for what had happened to me. The first thing I did was to call all the committees and groups I was involved with, and tell them that for a while I would not be able to work for them. Everything from the

NSPCC to the jumble sale committee would have to do without my efforts, because I had realised that I had to concentrate on my home and family.

Too often in the past I had put the children in the back of the car and told them to sit quietly and behave properly while I spent the morning ferrying people to hospital, church or library, considering my own 'righteousness' rather than the needs of my family. I would tell myself that when I had done all the 'duty' things I would have time to play with the children later, but of course by then I was so tired that I had no energy left for them, and would be more likely to snap and shout at them, or tell them to play quietly alone while I finished the housework. My church activities were leaving a trail of destruction in the family as I failed to meet the children's emotional needs, though I was punctilious in caring for their physical needs – good food, clean clothes, a tidy home.

So the first benefit was that I had more time for the family, and as the pressure of work eased, I had more energy for doing things with them. Interestingly, where I had previously felt trapped in the house, and resentful of Roy's freedom, I was now perfectly contented to stay at home. It was as if I had realised the value and importance in God's eyes of the job he had given me to do, and I understood what a privilege it was to be mother to four children and a wife to Roy.

In addition, I was never again afraid when I was alone in the house at night. In the past I would lie awake for hours, listening to every creak and rustle, expecting burglars, fire, earthquake – anything! Once I rang Roy in

Glasgow in the middle of the night to tell him that I could hear something tapping at the window – though what he was supposed to do about it at that distance, I can't imagine! Now I was filled with confidence and peace, as I knew that Jesus was with me all the time.

As time went on, other parts of me began to change, too. I stopped being so anxious and uptight about everything; I began to relax and enjoy life, and the dark clouds of depression lifted and vanished. One thing that improved was my ability to communicate with Roy. Before, whenever I felt depressed it was as though I pulled down a screen between us. I shut Roy out, and no matter what he did, whether he tried kindliness, sympathy, or sternness, it had no effect. Now, if I felt the cloud descending on me, I would go to him and say, 'Roy, I'm feeling ghastly,' and we would be able to talk about it. I no longer expected him to understand how I was feeling by telepathy, without being told about it, and I no longer added to my feelings of tiredness or depression by getting irritated and resentful.

It was about a month before Roy actually asked where I had been that day, and what I had been doing. Very hesitantly, because I was still rather afraid that he would be scornful, I told him.

'I went and had coffee with Tamara and she led me to Jesus. I confessed what a mess I'd made of everything and asked him to come into my life and make it his.'

Roy's response was immediate.

'Oh, thank goodness. I've been praying for years that you'd see the light and become a reasonable human being!'

I was immensely relieved. 'I was afraid to tell you,' I confessed, 'in case you laughed at me. I'd been so awful to you that I didn't think you'd believe me if I said things were going to be different.'

'I knew straight away, when you came back that day,' said Roy. 'When you went out, everything seemed so dark and depressing, it was as if the house was all grey and grimy and covered in cobwebs. When you came back, it was as if someone had redecorated it overnight!'

'Why didn't you say anything, then?' I asked.

'Well, I was afraid it might not last. But it has, hasn't it?'

It wasn't easy, though. My outlook might have changed, but my circumstances hadn't, and becoming a Christian does not inoculate us against the trials of everyday life. Sometimes I felt as though I was tiptoeing through a mine-field. If I lost my temper there was always the risk that he would say, 'I thought you were a Christian?' No one becomes perfect overnight, if ever, and I had to guard against many of my old habits. As I absorbed more teaching from the Bible, lots of my attitudes began to change. I began to recognise the wisdom of some of the things Roy had been patiently saying to me over the years: 'You never enjoy today because you're too worried about tomorrow' ('Therefore do not worry about tomorrow, for tomorrow will worry about itself' Matthew 6:34). I stopped being so anxious about punctuality and getting everyone organised when we were going anywhere. A while ago the children gave me a poster which illustrated this perfectly. It was a picture of hundreds of turkeys standing in a very orderly fashion, all looking up and facing the same way, and all looking absolutely identical. The caption read,

'Well, now that we're organized, what shall we do?' It was given with much love and a few giggles – I was only grateful that they were able to joke about it!

Another thing I took steps to alter was my deceitfulness. In the past I had never worried about telling the odd 'white lie' to wriggle out of something I didn't want to do, or to arrange things the way I wanted. For instance, I had always had trouble getting Antonia to go to bed earlier than the two older children (I put them to bed in order of age, very strictly, with no concessions). She would never settle down until the others were in bed, too, so I would get Daniel and Julia to pretend to go to bed with her, and whisper to them that they could come downstairs again once she was asleep. One night we heard Antonia coming downstairs again after about half an hour, and I hid the other two behind the sofa! She found them, of course, so that ploy didn't work again.

On another occasion I sent some chocolates to the mother of one of Ben's friends, who had kindly taken him to a football match. When she rang to thank me, Ben answered the phone: 'Oh, that's all right,' I heard him saying, 'we didn't have to pay for them. They were just some old ones we had left in the cupboard from Christmas!' Meanwhile I was making frantic signals to him and blushing furiously at his honesty. The point was that for a long time I didn't automatically tell the truth, and it was a while before I understood how bad an example this was for the children, and how important it was to be honest before God.

For many years all my dealings with my children were flawed by this sort of thing. Sometimes I knew that I had treated them unfairly or shouted at them unnecessarily, but I could never bring myself to say sorry. I thought that if I apologised to them I would lose their respect, so I would twist the circumstances to justify my conduct to them and to myself. Now I realised that I could confess anything I had done wrong to God, and be free of it. I didn't have to carry around a load of guilt all the time. Somehow this made it possible to admit when I was wrong to the children too, and say that I was sorry. To my surprise I did not lose their respect; rather, it seemed to draw us closer together, because they realised that Mum was not infallible – another release from the impossible standards I had been setting myself!

Over the months God began to put right some of the things that had been wrong in my life, and it was a joy to see how fast things improved. The children seemed more lighthearted and more secure, now that their mother was no longer snappy and unpredictable. Roy came home to a smile and a warm welcome instead of to a shrewish and tearful wife ('hatchet-faced' was how he described me!). I was feeling more in control of things than I had before; however, the next stage for me was learning to relinquish that control of my family life.

Tamara held regular meetings in her home, sometimes just for prayer, sometimes with speakers. My faith developed very rapidly with the help of this group; I saw answers to prayer, my own struggles were supported, and I received loving teaching from the others. On one occasion Stuart Reid, then assistant pastor from Gold Hill Baptist Church, came to speak on Ephesians 5 and other texts: 'You wives must submit to your husbands' leadership in the same way you submit to the Lord' (Ephesians 5:22, *Living Bible*). He said that the man's role was that of head of the family, and that he should make the ultimate decisions, and take responsibility for the discipline of the children.

I listened to his talk with growing impatience, and when he asked for questions afterwards, I fairly launched myself at him.

'How on earth can my husband take responsibility for the family discipline? He isn't even there most of the time! I'm the one who's on the spot and I have to deliver the discipline!'

'I'm not saying that a woman shouldn't discipline the children,' replied Stuart mildly, 'only that the big decisions about family life should be discussed between husband and wife and agreed between them. That gives security to the children because they know they can't play one off against the other.'

'And what if we can't decide?' I asked. 'What if we can't agree on the right solution?'

'Then the decision is ultimately the husband's. If it does turn out to be the wrong decision, he's far less likely to brood over it and feel guilty about it than a woman would. All she has to do is submit to his will – and remember not to say "I told you so" if it all goes wrong!'

'I'm not sure about all this,' I muttered. 'I didn't promise to obey when I got married. I don't think all this submission thing would fit into our marriage.'

'Well,' said Stuart, 'I suggest you go home and look it all up in the Bible. That's where you'll find out God's order for the family, and if you pray about it I think you'll find that it includes you.'

I went home armed with the Bible references and looked it all up. It wasn't drudgery for me, this study of the Bible – I was really anxious to find out more of the truth, even if I didn't much like what I found.

I realised that because Roy was away so much I had been forced into being fairly independent, and running the family unaided for long periods. However, I had then taken over the whole of Roy's task as father of the family, and insisted that the children were my business, because I had the main task of looking after them. I had usurped Roy's position as head of the family, when really we should have been sharing equally the task of making decisions about discipline, so that whatever I did was the outcome of a joint decision.

I had also grown to resent the easy-going role into which I had forced Roy; he would arrive home from lengthy trips abroad, laden with presents for the children he'd missed for so long. I would feel angry that he was seen as the warm, sunny, gift-giver, while I was saddled with being mean Mummy who was always saying 'no'. I began to understand that a great deal of imbalance in our family life stemmed from this issue of submission, and we were going to have to work through it together.

I was very keen to start putting things right at once, so that weekend I decided that I would no longer take the reins of discipline in the family, but let Roy take charge. After breakfast on Sunday I watched as the children started bickering, chasing each other round the table and knocking a pile of magazines to the floor. I waited for Roy to do his manly thing and send them all to their rooms, but he went on peacefully reading the Sunday papers as chaos reigned around him. That was when I realised that you had to be open-minded about the response; submission did not mean making your husband do what you wanted him to!

I think that on that occasion I did intervene and put a stop to the chaos, but it was clear that we needed to discuss the whole issue. It was a new idea for Roy, too; he had been happy for me to take over the discipline when he was away, though he admitted that he did sometimes think I was too strict with the children. It was obvious that all the discipline needed to be agreed between us, even if I was the one who administered it. As Roy pointed out, 'I can't come in after a week away, and suddenly switch on being angry with the children for something they did last week!'

At around the same time I came across a verse in the Bible about appearances: 'Don't be concerned about the outward beauty that depends on jewellery, or beautiful clothes, or hair arrangement. Be beautiful inside, in your hearts, with the lasting charm of a gentle and a quiet spirit which is so precious to God' (1 Peter 3:3–4, *Living Bible*). I found this to be a great release for me. I always felt that I ought to look smart, and I wanted Roy to be proud of me, but this verse seemed to say that I didn't need to live up to the 'glamorous show-business' image, and that as long as Roy wasn't ashamed of how I looked, then I didn't need extravagant clothes or jewels.

At last I was able to see the difference between being a Christian and merely 'going to church'. We still went to church as a family, but now I was looking for the answers to specific questions, bringing what I learned on Sunday into my life during the week. I had grasped the great good news that I didn't have to struggle to earn favour with God, because he already loved me. And I now knew that I didn't have to exhaust myself trying to be 'good' or 'righteous', because that was a lost cause: on my own I could never meet God's standards of holiness. But that didn't matter, because Jesus had died for my sins, so they were wiped out in God's eyes. All that remained for me to do was to attempt to live my life in the new way, in Jesus' way, guided by the Holy Spirit in everything I did.

Life still had its ups and downs, of course, but now Roy and I were working together, praying and seeking God's will for our children and our family life. All four children were a great joy to us, especially in the faith we all shared, and I was so glad that as they grew up we continued to love and support each other. We never expected that Roy, the fit, strong father-figure in our family, would be struck down by cancer, and when those dark days came, we needed each other more than ever.

3
Dark Days

Some six months before Roy was taken ill I wondered if God was preparing me for a time of testing. I had been thanking God for all my blessings, when a strange thought came into my mind: what would I do if my wonderful life became difficult, if something awful happened? Would I still be able to trust the Lord if everything was bleak? Could God trust me with the bad times as well as the good? I hoped so. I hoped my faith was not so weak as to falter at the first hurdle. Yet the thought returned again and again. It put me in mind of Simon Peter, when Jesus said to him repeatedly, 'Peter, do you love me?'

That summer we took a holiday in Australia. We had an amazing time, basking in the tropical heat, sightseeing and even snorkelling on the Great Barrier Reef. Above all, it was good to have time for each other; to do things together without having to plan around two busy schedules. We realised that this was indeed a God-given holiday, a chance to refresh and enrich our relationship. As we lazed in the sun, we both reflected on how contented we were to be together. I had the chance to catch up on a lot of reading and study, and some thinking and prayer, too. During that time I wrote down some of my thoughts in a notebook; in particular, that my great desire was to make Roy glad that he'd married me, for the rest of our lives. It seemed rather a far-fetched idea, in a way; yet I was increasingly aware of what a faithful, wonderful husband he'd been to me for almost thirty years. Our marriage had not always run smoothly, and we had our share of difficulties and differences. I was so thankful that even before I came to know God as I do now, I had still believed firmly in the sanctity of our marriage vows and our complete fidelity to each other. In the hard times that dutiful adherence to our vows had probably kept us together; I was glad we had weathered those times, and coming to know Jesus as my saviour transformed our marriage and my life.

A few days after our return to England Roy woke one night with an agonising headache. When he asked me to call the doctor I knew something must be seriously wrong – he usually shrugged off any minor ailments as unimportant. Anyway, he was hardly ever ill – he was one of the fittest people I knew.

The duty doctor came and gave him a thorough examination, and said that she couldn't find anything obviously wrong. His heart was all right – I'd specially asked about that – but he was still clearly in such pain that she thought he ought to be admitted to hospital for observation. I didn't want to drive with him in that state, so she called an ambulance.

It was typical of Roy that when the ambulance arrived he was sitting on the side of the bed, clutching his head in his hands; yet as soon as the ambulance men came in and began tucking him into a chair to carry him outside, he started laughing and joking with them. I felt quite exasperated – surely they'd think that if he was fit enough to joke, he must be making a fuss about nothing! But as he was lifted into the ambulance I looked at his face, pinched and white with pain, and my heart lurched again. Something was badly wrong with him, and I was powerless to help.

As I followed the ambulance in my car I was praying that everything would be all right. When I arrived I was directed to Roy's cubicle, and I found him propped up in bed, wired up to some alarming-looking machines which were monitoring his heart. However, he looked ridiculously fit, tanned and healthy from the Australian sun and laughing and chatting with the nurses. I had the strange feeling that everything was unreal – it couldn't really be happening.

After a while, Roy was moved on a trolley up to the ward, and put into bed in a side ward. The nurse in charge suggested that I should go home and get some sleep, and Roy should sleep too.

By the time I got home it was about five o'clock; still dark, but I remember hearing a bird begin to sing in the garden. I didn't go back to bed – as I usually rise at about six it didn't seem worth it.

At nine o'clock the telephone rang; to my surprise it was Roy.

'Fiona? Can you come and get me, please? They're discharging me! Yes, I'm fine – well, still a bit of a headache, but nothing like it was. How soon can you get here?'

43

I fetched him home, he went to bed and fell asleep. I went to church and about my usual Sunday activities, looking in on him from time to time, and taking up some lunch and supper. He was reading or writing letters, and the migraine medication the hospital had given him seemed to be working. The nightmare was over – just one of those random things, I thought. It probably wouldn't happen again. Maybe it was migraine after all.

However, that night the same thing happened – he woke at about three a.m. in terrible pain, and paced the room holding his head. This time I was more confident, because I knew that the hospital had already checked him for epilepsy and heart trouble, so I tried to calm him down. We didn't want to bother the doctor again, after what had seemed to be a kind of 'false alarm', so we hung on until seven the next morning, when we thought that at least the doctor would have had a good night's sleep. This time our own GP came out to see him, and gave him a massive injection of migraine medication. It didn't work.

He was in pain all that day, and that night. By Tuesday afternoon he was haggard with pain and lack of sleep; he said he felt claustrophobic, as though he was encased in his own body and unable to escape. He could neither sit nor lie still, but paced up and down the room, round and round the house, endlessly, all day and all night. By Wednesday he was in such agony that we contacted the doctor again, and he arranged for Roy to see a neurologist.

Roy spent a week in hospital. I visited him every day for some hours in the afternoon, and again in the evening if

44

no friends were there. In fact he slept a lot of the time, partly because of the painkilling drugs he was taking. Although he was able to think clearly when he was awake, his speech sounded oddly slurred, as though he had been drinking. Every possible test was run – x-rays, blood tests, a lumbar puncture and a brain scan.

When I visited on the fourth evening, Roy had some good news.

'Guess what!' he said cheerfully. 'They think they've found something positive. The last set of blood tests showed that I haven't got enough sodium in my blood.'

'What on earth does that mean?' I asked. 'I didn't know you were supposed to have any!'

'No, well, neither did I. But I got the doctor to explain it. It's the fluid balance in the blood that's the problem; it may mean a special diet, and restricting fluids, that's all.'

I was delighted. Something that could be corrected just by a diet didn't sound too bad. 'So when can you come home?'

'It shouldn't be long. They just want to set up the diet and check that it works for a couple of days.'

'Great. Maybe it's just a virus or an allergy or something that's caused it,' I mused.

Roy looked thoughtful. 'Yes, I said the same thing. They just said they didn't know the answer to that one yet.'

On Thursday, eight days after his admission, Roy came home and went back to work. He felt rather defeated because for the first time in his entire career he had had to cancel a show, and he was very anxious to get back to normal. The headaches had cleared up with the restricted fluid diet, though he was armed with a battery of painkill-ers, just in case. His schedule was just as busy as ever: he was planning a trip to the USA for Anglia Television in the spring, to make a series of religious programmes in which he would be travelling around looking at Christianity at work in various places – among the home-less in New York, Gospel singers in New Orleans, etc. He spent a lot of time with the producer, deciding on the content of the programmes and working out the itinerary.

In the middle of all this, the hospital suggested that he give up the low fluid diet as an experiment, since he seemed to be so stable. The monitoring showed that the condition of his blood relapsed immediately, and he was called to St Mary's, Paddington, for a morning of tests.

I still wasn't particularly concerned. I was convinced that the strange sodium loss was due to something every-day, like a virus or an allergy, and that it would eventu-ally clear up. Roy submitted to some x-rays and a scan, came home and got on with some work.

The next morning the telephone rang at 7.30. It was the specialist at St Mary's, asking Roy to go back immediately to repeat the x-rays, as they were not happy with them. I tried to carry on with my day as usual, but this time I was beginning to question: could it possibly be something serious? Why else would they call back so early, insisting that Roy must repeat the test that day? I was glad when Roy got home at lunch time, and I could ask him what happened.

'Nothing much,' he told me. 'They just did the x-rays again. The only thing was – while they were looking at the results, one of the doctors asked me if I smoked. I said no, but I've worked a lot in smoky atmospheres. You know what they're thinking . . .'

I was dumbfounded. 'It can't be! You've never smoked in your life! It can't be – lung cancer. Can it?'

I'd said the word. For the first time I realised why the word 'cancer' is so avoided, why so many people try not to think about it, refuse to say it. As a clinical condition it is an illness like any other. As something that may possibly attack someone you love, it suddenly seemed like a nightmare.

After that, once the possibility had been voiced, time seemed to stand still. On one level life went on as normal; I cleaned the house, visited friends, helped at church, cooked meals and ate them. On another level, at the back of my mind there was a continual debate. Roy can't have cancer. He's never smoked in his life. But passive smoking is supposed to be almost as bad. All those nights in smoky nightclubs. But surely he couldn't play a trumpet the way he does if there was something wrong with his lungs? He can't have cancer . . .

A bronchoscopy was arranged for Sunday, and I drove Roy to the Nuffield hospital after lunch (which he wasn't allowed to eat) and collected him that evening. The operation involved passing a small tube down into the lung and removing piece of tissue for testing. The patient has to be heavily sedated, though not completely anaesthetised, and Roy could remember nothing of the ordeal.

'You were great,' said one of the doctors as we were leaving. 'You were telling us jokes the whole time!'

'You might have written them down, then,' retorted

47

Roy. 'They might have been new material, I could use them again!'

The results were due on Tuesday.

In some ways that day was the most difficult of all for me. I had hoped that the call would come early in the morning, but nothing happened. It was my day for helping with the crèche at church, while a meeting was going on. Usually I like to have a cup of tea as soon as I arrive, but that day I could not swallow anything; I felt as though there was a lump in my throat. However, we had a job to do and I didn't want to disrupt the routine, so I didn't tell anyone what was going on. I had to be my normal bright, cheerful self – though inside I felt completely numb. I wasn't worrying; I just felt as though I was suspended in time, waiting endlessly to be told the news I was dreading.

That afternoon the specialist rang through to Roy, and asked him to go up to the Nuffield to see him. He refused to discuss the test results over the phone, but when Roy said, 'What about my trip to America?', he replied, 'I don't think you'll be going to America.'

I suppose we knew then, really, that the news was going to be bad, but we still had more time to get through, more waiting to do.

Roy wanted to go alone to the hospital, and in any case we were expecting a friend, Dave Foster, so I had to stay at home. Roy was doing the voice-over for a video Dave was making, and the only possible time it could be done was that very evening, as Dave was flying to Moscow the next morning.

When Dave arrived Roy was still out, so I explained

where he was. Dave looked shocked and offered to leave, but I knew that Roy would want to keep his promise to finish the job. We waited together, hardly speaking, till we heard the front door open and Roy came in.

We both jumped up as he came into the room.

'What's the news?' I asked. Even if one part of me had been hoping that it was all a terrible mistake, one look at Roy's face told me the truth.

'It's the worst possible,' he said quietly. 'It's the fastest-growing cancer there is. I have three months without treatment; maybe six months with treatment.'

There was nothing we could do, nothing we could say. Poor Dave was compelled to be in on this trauma; he could see that we needed to be alone, to try to come to terms with the most devastating situation we had ever faced, yet here was Roy resolutely keeping the lid on his emotions, and setting off in the most businesslike way to get his script. They shut themselves in the dining-room to work, and I went to the kitchen to answer any phone calls so that the bell would not disturb them.

I had known it was coming, this news, ever since that first hint from the x-rays, yet now it was certain I felt deadened with the shock. My body felt heavy, cold and numb, and I leaned against the radiator for warmth. My thoughts went round and round in circles, until I reached out instinctively in prayer.

'Lord, what's going on? Why is this happening? What are you doing to us? What's the purpose of all this? What are you telling us through this?' The questions went on and on, not making much sense, but reaching out to the Father I loved and trusted, and who I knew had the power to bring us through. I didn't feel angry with God, and I didn't feel that it was a burden he had designed and placed upon us; I just felt weak with shock, and held out my hands for the reassurance of his love.

I stood there shivering for a while but soon I began to feel calmer. I began to feel the reassurance I'd been longing for, and I knew that I would eventually have peace – though whether through Roy's healing, or through his death, I had no idea.

It seemed a very long time before Roy and Dave finished their work in the dining-room, and then we had to watch the whole video through to check it. Afterwards Dave escaped as fast as he could.

When we were alone at last, we held each other tightly and burst into tears. We faced the truth together and wept, letting go all the dreadful tension of the last weeks. We knew that there were worse times ahead of us, but in the shadow of sudden illness, you realise just how precious every moment together really is. Suddenly the prayer I had prayed on holiday – 'Lord, let me make Roy glad he married me, for the rest of our lives' – seemed unbearably poignant. How long, in fact, would we have?

The knowledge that Roy had cancer changed our lives: it was painful to realise that suddenly we had no future. All our immediate plans were dashed; Roy's trip to America would have to be cancelled, and everything from now on would revolve around the slim hope offered by treatment. We cried together, and talked, and cried some more.

Telling the children was difficult, too. Benjamin and Antonia were living at home, but Roy went to London to tell Julia, and we rang Daniel who was in Norway. 'The stupid thing is that I feel so well,' Roy kept saying. 'It's so hard to believe that you can have a terminal illness and feel perfectly all right.'

On Wednesday evening we had a visit from Jim Graham, our minister, and Peter Falconer, one of the church elders. Jim came straight to the point. 'I was very upset when Fiona told me about your illness, Roy. But this evening I've come in my professional capacity, as your pastor, to pray with you.'

We all sat down, and Jim went on, 'Look what it says in the Bible: "Is any one of you sick? He should call the elders of the church to pray over him and anoint him with oil in the name of the Lord. And the prayer offered in faith will make the sick person well; the Lord will raise him up. If he has sinned, he will be forgiven. Therefore confess your sins to each other and pray for each other so that you may be healed. The prayer of a righteous man is powerful and effective."' (James 5:14–16)

We prayed together, and then Jim put oil on Roy's forehead and we all laid hands on him. We didn't feel anything spectacular happening, but it was very loving and simple. Jim and Peter did not stay long, as it was getting late and they had been out all evening. The extraordinary thing was that when we were in bed that night, we both realised that we were talking without emotion, and the depression and turmoil we had felt all afternoon had left us. It was as if we had accepted the promise of healing, and all was well and everything had returned to normal. We both felt very peaceful and were able to sleep soundly.

Three days after his diagnosis, Roy went into hospital

for his first chemotherapy treatment, and we began to settle into a pattern: on the first week he had a 24-hour treatment, on the second it was only 12 hours, the third week it was 24 hours again. Before each treatment he had to have an x-ray and a blood test, because the drugs which were killing off the cancer cells were also killing off his healthy cells. On one occasion his blood count had not recovered sufficiently, so he had to have a rest from the treatment, and on another he needed a blood transfusion as he was getting so weak.

It was during the third week that Anglia TV put out a Press Release saying that Roy had been replaced in their forthcoming series about the United States, and of course, all the reporters wanted to know why. That Thursday the phone started ringing at 9 p.m. and went on all evening. Over and over again we explained what was happening, until we felt like answering machines ourselves! At last, at 2 a.m., peace descended and the phone stopped ringing.

'Thank goodness that's over,' I said. 'Now they've all got their stories and we can have some peace.' We'd had some experience of this sort of thing before – just occasionally when Roy was in the news, there would be a flurry of press activity until all the reporters had filed their stories for the next day's newspapers, and then it would all be over.

I went out the next morning and got home about noon. To my amazement the house was under siege: the road and the drive were both full of parked cars; when I got into the house the living room was full of reporters, and when I finally reached the kitchen, the sink was full of coffee cups! Roy and Benjamin had spent the whole morning coping with reporters, giving them coffee and answering questions; most of them had been very pleasant, though some were both thoughtless and demanding. This continued for days, until I began seriously to worry whether it was going to be too tiring for Roy.

I wondered many times about the enormous amount of press attention at that time, and also about the tremendous focusing of prayer by Christians everywhere. Why should we be so privileged? I now believe that it was all part of God's plan for bringing glory to His name. The day after Roy's diagnosis I had felt that God was saying to me, 'Stand back and see what I am doing. I will bring great glory to my name through this.' I wondered what the purpose could possibly be, but now I know that the way Roy faced illness and death with unswerving faith has inspired many people to look again at the promises of Jesus. They saw someone who was not spared suffering, but who still drew strength and joy from the love of God.

Thousands of people wrote to us – one letter was addressed to 'Roy Castle, Entertainer, Huddersfield, Buckinghamshire'! The postman took to delivering in a van because his bicycle could not cope with the bags of mail. It was an exhausting and time-consuming job trying to answer all these letters personally, but it gave us a daily goal, trying to keep up with it all. Some people wrote long letters recounting their own experiences, glad to share and aiming to help and offer hope. One woman wrote this, which I found very helpful: 'Jesus did not come into the world to stop suffering, nor to explain it, nor to take it away, but to fill it with his presence.'

Some of the most touching cards were those hand-made by children in an oncology (cancer) ward in a hospital. Childish drawings of Roy doing *Record Breakers* or of their own hospital beds, with scrawled writing saying things like 'Go for it, Roy' 'Don't die – fight for us'. They were so moving, we wept many times over them. These children had their whole lives in prospect. How did they, and their parents, feel? When I looked at those cards I felt thankful for the full lives we had already led.

Often in the early days I would suggest that Roy should turn down interviews or appearances, partly so that he could conserve his strength. Roy would reply with a shrug of the shoulders:

'It's all in the Lord's hands. He's engineering all this and there must be a reason for it.' For many years he had been asking the Lord to use him, and he had always received the answer, 'Just wait.' Now he realised that he had been given a platform to speak out against the dangers of smoking with great authority, with the added influence of the doctors' conclusion that passive smoking can cause lung cancer, backed up by his own experience as a non-smoker with the disease. Later, as he returned to health, he took on a great deal of charity work to support cancer research. He had always wanted to do something so real that no one could doubt the truth of what he was saying – but I don't think he ever expected the answer to that prayer to come through suffering from cancer.

4
Give Us This Day

Gradually the treatment began to take effect, and Roy began to suffer the side effects. First of all, just as we had been warned, his hair began to fall out – not in small amounts, but in handfuls. One night he came out of the bathroom in his dressing gown and called to Antonia,

'Hey, Anto, come up here with your camera, will you? I want a record of this little lot!'

Antonia came upstairs, and there all along the sides of the bath were little clumps of Roy's hair, carefully arranged for a snapshot.

'Gives a whole new meaning to "Wash and Go", doesn't it?' he grinned.

Other side effects were more distressing. First his nails grew thin and brittle, and stopped growing; then his skin became increasingly thin. The chemicals which were stopping the cancer cells from growing and dividing were having the same effect on his healthy cells. The skin at the ends of his fingers began to split, and it was painful for him to pick things up.

'It's a shame my hands are so painful,' he said with a wry smile. 'I'd make a fantastic burglar at the moment: I've got no fingerprints!' It was true: the skin had worn away and not been replaced, and the whorled pattern had disappeared. He had to wear special fine rubber gloves to protect his nerve-endings.

Perhaps the worst, though, were the mouth ulcers. Eventually I had to blend all his food like a baby's, and after several weeks he could manage nothing but juices.

One of the problems with the chemotherapy was that the effects were patchy – Roy could feel terribly ill one day, and relatively well the next. It was hard to predict how he would feel at any time, so we could never really plan anything properly.

On one occasion he had agreed to appear at an 'Aerobathon' – a massive aerobics class at the Earls Court Exhibition Centre. The day before, Roy was so ill that he could hardly lift his head off the pillow.

'Roy, you just won't be able to get there tomorrow,' I said to him. 'Let me ring and cancel it – the organisers will be sure to understand. No one can possibly blame you for not being there.'

To my amazement Roy, usually the mildest of men, sat up in a fury.

'Why can't you leave me alone?' he shouted. 'It's my life and my business. Just don't interfere with me. Why don't you get out of the house and never come back?'

I rushed out of the room in tears, and sat downstairs trying to make sense of what was happening. Was it the drugs making him like this, or just the tension of feeling so ill?

After a few minutes the phone began to ring. When I picked it up, it was Roy on the other end, calling from the bedroom!

'I'm sorry I shouted at you. I don't know what got into me – it was just as if I was standing outside myself watching, but I couldn't stop . . . Please forgive me!'

After that, I was careful to watch what I said and did, and tried to be aware of what kind of mood he was in. I could tell that Roy was being cautious, too, watching himself for another outbreak. Most of the time he was appreciative of all my efforts, but occasionally he would snap at me. I began to see when I was irritating him, by fussing around trying to make him comfortable, or by trying to protect him from doing too much. It was difficult for both of us; it was so out of character for him to be irritable that I would find it hard not to cry. It was unlike me to be so emotional, too, but I couldn't help it. I tried to hide my feelings and went on being very positive for his sake. I became sure that it was the drugs which made him so unreasonable once he had an idea fixed in his mind.

Some things were particularly difficult for me to deal with. I loved my husband dearly, and it was agonising to be beside him and watch him suffer. There is a particular kind of pain in being the carer in this situation, and it was only my faith in God which helped me to see my way through these dark days.

On the Sunday before Easter Roy was too ill to go to church, so I went alone. I was praying as I walked along:

'Why, Lord? Isn't it enough that Roy has cancer and has to go through this awful treatment? Why does he have to

57

suffer all these side effects and feel so ill? Couldn't you at least heal those?'

As I prayed it was as if God showed me Jesus in the Garden of Gethsemane. He showed me that Jesus had asked to be spared the pain and horror, the anguish and the indignity – but yet he continued to say that it was the Father's will, not his own human will that he wanted to fulfil. God said, 'See my Son. He did not sidestep the pain: he walked towards it and went through it.'

That was enough to stop me from complaining. Roy himself had said, 'Whatever I am going through is nothing compared with what Jesus went through. And I need to experience everything other cancer patients suffer, to be able to identify with them.'

The truth was that looking after Roy was tiring, both emotionally and physically. One of my many faults, and one which I suspect I share with many people, is that I am very independent. I love to give of my time and energy to others, but I'm not so good at being on the receiving end. In the early days of Roy's cancer, most of the friends who phoned us said, 'If there's anything we can do to help, just ask.' If they were Christians, we simply asked them to pray; otherwise we said thank you and that we would let them know. I know that if our positions had been reversed, I would have made the same offer, and I would have been pleased and flattered if the person had accepted, and asked me to do any small service which would enable me to express my love and caring. However, in fact I usually found it hard to think of anything which other people could help with. Perhaps it's just that when we're under stress it takes almost more energy to delegate a job than to do it ourselves. I now think that perhaps the best kind of offer of help would have been a specific one, so that I didn't have to stop and try to think about what needed doing. The person who turns up with a home-made cake, or who commandeers the kitchen and unobtrusively does the ironing or the washing up without making an issue of it, is a real help to the carer.

I am sure that there are important lessons for us all to learn about how to offer sympathy to each other, and how to do it in a sensitive way. In particular, the role of the carer can sometimes be a lonely one, when all attention is focused (quite rightly) on the sufferer and his treatment. This is where church fellowships can come into their own with a varied range of ministries, from physical help where that is needed, to emotional support for someone who occasionally simply needs to let some of their feelings out. Not all Christians, however well-meaning, are good at this kind of sensitivity.

In spite of the stress of Roy's illness, I never seemed to suffer the kind of depression I had sometimes felt in the past. I always knew that I could take my troubles to the Lord. The security and confidence that gave me enabled me to be cheerful and buoyant most of the time, and we laughed a great deal through all the inconveniences and difficulties of the illness. One well-meaning correspondent wrote to me, 'You don't realise what a privilege it is for you to serve Roy at this time.' This immediately became a family joke, and when I brought Roy his breakfast, he would say,

'Thank you, darling. I hope you realise what a privilege it is for you to bring me my breakfast!'

Many of Roy's show-business friends are comics; when they visited or telephoned it was hard to believe that they were commiserating with a very sick man – the jokes would fly thick and fast and everyone would be laughing together. I'm sure that the laughter they brought with them did Roy more good than almost anything else. 'It's taught me a lesson,' Roy said to me one day. 'You know, before all this happened, if ever I heard that someone was ill, I'd think, "What a shame," but I probably wouldn't do anything about it. I wouldn't even have expected that someone who was ill would want to hear from me. But now I realise just how important it is. I'm so grateful when friends call in or write or phone – it really brightens up the day!'

We were immensely grateful for all the interest and concern and love that seemed to surround us. Both strangers and friends wrote and telephoned and showed that they cared in many ways, sending everything from flowers to advice. One piece of wise counsel, for which we were always grateful, came from our pastor, Jim Graham.

'Now that so many people know that Roy is ill,' he said, 'you will receive lots of comments, advice and information from many sources. Some of it will be helpful, some of it will be unhelpful, and both sorts will come from other Christians. I want to reassure you that whatever the future holds for you, I and the whole church fellowship are standing with you and rooting for you.' This proved to be a real support to us, as with this forewarning we were not so troubled as we might have been when the odder letters and suggestions started arriving. Several people wrote to Roy and told him that his illness was due to some unconfessed sin in his life, and that the evil inherent in show business was the cause.

Other suggestions were equally unhelpful, though well-intentioned. For instance, we knew from the specialists that Roy could expect to start losing his hair after the third week of chemotherapy: the hair becomes brittle and breaks off just above the follicle. A few Christian friends were convinced that this did not have to be the case; they were sure that if we prayed, God would preserve Roy's hair, and they said that they knew of other cases where this had happened. When his hair fell out, right on cue, I felt that people would think that I didn't have enough faith. Then we heard that only certain types of medication have this effect on the hair. The instances where the 'faithful' didn't suffer hair loss could equally have been the result of different drugs. Even as I felt released from my feelings of guilt, I began to see how silly the whole thing was. Why should we set up hoops for our prayer lives to jump through? God isn't trying to play games with us, or set us targets of this much or that much faith.

Often as Christians we become so introspective that anything can become an occasion for feelings of guilt. Am I feeling low, or depressed? Then at once I add to my burden by feeling guilty as well, because 'Christians should be full of joy', so I must be lacking in faith. In fact, it may not be faith that is lacking so much as a good night's sleep or a square meal! After all, we are physical creatures as well as spiritual ones. I have learned not to be swayed too much by my feelings, and not to mistake temporary states of health or mood for spiritual crises.

Roy's security and simple faith in God were an enormous help to me: often I would study and pray and agonise my way into some new idea, only to find that Roy had been there for years, patiently waiting for me to catch up!

Our experience of the Holy Spirit was rather like this. Before I became a Christian I didn't understand about him at all; I usually referred to him as 'it', and couldn't quite see the role of the third Person of the Trinity. After I had become a Christian I had several dreams about the Holy Spirit, from which I would wake up aware that someone had been with me, but still not understanding much. I didn't like to speak to Roy about it, as I was still being very cautious in case he thought I was becoming a religious maniac! I questioned Tamara and she promised that we would get together and pray about it.

'Actually,' she added, 'I don't think you really need to. I believe that you are already filled with the Spirit – I've seen you several times showing the sort of wisdom you couldn't naturally show. That wisdom is one of the gifts of the Spirit. But don't worry, I'll explain it all when I see you.'

Meanwhile, with a spark of inspiration, I had decided that it was all very well ringing up Tamara with my questions, but what about ringing up God? So I found a book on the subject (*The Holy Spirit and You* by Dennis Bennett), and got down on my knees for a conversation with God.

'Lord, if you have filled me with your Spirit, please show me. I'm a very new Christian, and I need a sign of confirmation that this is true. Please give me the gift of "tongues".'

As I prayed and praised God, I found a strange word came into my mouth. As soon as I had spoken it, I thought, 'How silly – it must just be me making it up.' Somehow the idea struck me as funny and I began to giggle. As I laughed, more words came, and there I was, speaking in tongues and laughing at the same time. If anyone had seen or heard me I'm sure they would have thought that I was crazy, talking in the strange language the Lord had given me, in between giggles.

The next day I phoned Tamara. 'You were right,' I said, 'I've already got it!'

However, when I finally spoke to Roy about it, he was his usual calm self. He, too, had been filled with the Holy Spirit but he had never spoken in tongues. 'Well, I don't need a sign that he's in me, do I?' he said. One of Roy's spiritual gifts was an astounding ability to go straight to the heart of a problem, and a wonderful wisdom in dealing with people, together with a great assurance of faith.

Throughout his illness I was grateful for that simple, straightforward faith. There were no complications in it, just continuous supplication to the throne of God – for protection during the medication and treatment, for skill and wisdom for the medical profession, and for God's healing to flow through these channels.

This is another area where some Christians seem to have differing views. I have met people who say that they refuse to call a doctor if a member of the family is ill, but rely only on prayer. They suggest that to rely on human medication is a sign of a lack of faith.

This was a troubling area for me, because I believe in

God's ability to heal people directly, and I have witnessed people being healed. I consulted a wise pastor friend about this, and asked him if it showed a lack of faith to rely on medicine rather than on miraculous 'divine healing'. He replied, 'Unless you get a clear word from the Lord specifically saying that God will heal in this case through a miracle, you should not depend upon it.'

I found this a great comfort, and I am sure that we did the right thing in choosing to let God heal Roy through the medical profession. In fact, Roy refused to say 'God has healed me.' He knew that the cancer might recur – and what would that do to the faith of anyone who had trusted his words? We knew that God might heal him for a while only, and then call him to himself in his own time. Roy always said that God was in control, but that the doctors' skill was also a gift of God.

'We're in God's hands,' he would say. 'We're not doubting; we're trusting totally that God has a plan and a purpose in this. Anyone who wants to dispute it can deal with him!' We felt that we were giving God the glory when we showed that we were trusting him, whether or not Roy was healed.

After the course of chemotherapy had finished, Roy had a short break and then the radiotherapy started. Because this was an outpatient procedure, he would meet other patients in the reception area, waiting for their turn in the treatment room. They chatted among themselves and it soon became clear that it was rather like a cancer patients' club meeting – enlivened, no doubt, by Roy's humour. One man said that he was rather sorry that his course of radiotherapy finished before Roy's, as he enjoyed their afternoons so much!

After his final session of radiotherapy there was a three-week break, and then he had another scan and bronchoscopy to test his lung tissue. I was so sure of Roy's healing by then that it was a real shock when the doctors told us that they had found some cancer cells still in his lung. There was no evidence that they were growing, but it meant that Roy was by no means declared clear of cancer. I had been all ready to shout to the world that the Lord had healed Roy, and the news was a shocking blow. For several days I felt very depressed and bitterly disappointed.

That was when I realised that I was making too many assumptions about God's plan for us. I had to acknowledge once again that God's ways are higher than our ways (Isaiah 55), and that his ways are perfect. It was not for me to dictate the way in which God would be glorified through Roy's illness, nor for me to say when the whole episode was to end so that I could close the book on it. What I really wanted was for it all to be over so that we could slip back into ordinary, everyday life – and, of course, into all our old ways of taking life, health and all its blessings for granted.

Instead, I still had to trust God for each day as it came, enjoying each as a precious gift. I was reminded once again that we have to hold on to God for our daily walk, not just at times of crisis but at all times. And this, in its turn, made me look closely at my everyday life and whether I was fulfilling God's will for me in the place where he wanted me to be. It is difficult for me to write about these things, because I have been fortunate in my life, and we have seldom been very short of money. Yet I see so many people who put all their energies into earning more and more money to obtain more and more material things, and I know that this seldom brings them contentment. If people do not have a sense of self-worth, they put their trust in material things as an alternative, as though owning more possessions can prove that they are valuable, successful people.

Roy always said that although he came from a very poor family, still, while he was growing up he always felt like a king. His parents made him feel valued for himself, and so he grew up with confidence and self-respect, which no amount of money can buy. Of course, even if we have not been fortunate in the support of our family, and have grown up feeling uncertain and inadequate, there is a sure remedy. There is one person to whom we are always important, who will always love us no matter what, and in whose eyes we have infinite worth. 'God loved the world so much that he gave his only Son so that anyone who believes in him shall not perish but have eternal life' (John 3:16, *Living Bible*). Putting our trust in owning material things is pointless, because in the end they are not important, and when we die we must leave them behind. 'Don't store up treasures here on earth where they can erode away or may be stolen. Store them in heaven where they will never lose their value, and are safe from thieves. If your profits are in heaven, your heart will be there too' (Matthew 6:19–21, *Living Bible*). The true riches are in knowing God, and if we are doing his will we are storing our treasure in heaven.

5
Journey's End

After his treatment in 1992 Roy seemed to be restored to perfect health, and went back to a full schedule of work for nearly a year – a very happy year which we lived and enjoyed to the full. Every healthy day was a bonus.

However, during the summer of 1993 he developed a persistent cough which neither antibiotics nor asthma treatments seemed able to clear, and we began the cycle of tests and visits to doctors once more. By the end of November he was in great pain and unable to swallow any solid food, and it became clear that the cancer had returned. This time the specialist was gloomy.

'The prognosis is poorer this time,' he said. 'The cancer has started up again, and we can't subject you to treatment of such intensity again. My advice is to go home and enjoy Christmas.'

Nevertheless he prescribed some chemotherapy pills and Roy's determined spirit took over. He took the pills and insisted on fulfilling his promise and opening in

Pickwick which was playing for the Christmas season in Birmingham.

Both the cast of *Pickwick* and the public were immensely supportive, and Roy's part had been cut down so that he would not get too tired. Usually he catnapped in the dressing room between his entrances, and on one occasion he awoke with a start to hear the backstage tannoy calling 'Roy Castle on stage *now!*' Terrified of missing his cue Roy jumped up still half asleep, hit every wall of the dressing room and then walked into a closed door! The chemotherapy pills often left him confused, and when he forgot his lines he just made them up until the other members of the cast dragged him back to the script. I think they all enjoyed the diversions, and they certainly helped him along with great good humour.

We had a strange Christmas that year. The specialist had told us to gather all the family together, as he thought that Roy was unlikely to live into the New Year. Our daughter Julia was working in Peru, but since Roy was managing much better than anyone had expected, we decided not to call her home. She was due home for a holiday in February anyway. The rest of us enjoyed ourselves, and as Roy was working until the day before Christmas Eve I had been unable to do any preparation. I just called in at Marks and Spencer, bought an entirely instant Christmas dinner, packed it into the car and drove it home! It was a remarkably restful time.

After Christmas we returned to Birmingham for the rest of the run. Roy was determined not to give in however ill he felt, so when we were told that the show was closing unexpectedly it was shocking but welcome news. The theatre had gone bankrupt, which meant that it had to cease trading immediately – the run ended with a matinee performance and that was that. In fact Roy was so ill that evening that I was really worried about driving him home to Gerrards Cross; I was mentally planning escape routes on the way, in case we had to stop and find a hospital.

Once again we visited the doctor, and once again medication was prescribed which seemed to put things right for a time. We were back on the old switchback of treatment, with improvements and side-effects swinging us up and down. However, we always felt that God was our secret weapon. The doctors, for all their expertise, care and concern, did not include God in their calculations; we did. We never claimed miracles, nor did we ever claim that Roy was or would be healed. We simply said that we could trust God whatever the circumstances; here were the circumstances back again, and we were still trusting.

It wasn't until May that the next phase of the illness declared itself. We had travelled to Manchester to speak at a Christian meeting, and were sitting around a dining table with some other guests. Roy was idly drumming his two index fingers on the edge of the table to some private beat inside his head, when he became aware that his left hand felt rather sluggish. He kept up with the cheerful conversation around the table, but from time to time he tested his fingers; there was no doubt that his left hand wasn't working properly. He told me quietly so as not to alarm the other guests; my stomach lurched but I managed to keep smiling.

'There's probably a logical explanation for it,' I assured

him in an undertone. 'Perhaps you're tired. It'll be all right tomorrow.' But as we drove home that night our hearts were heavy. Roy recalled a story he had heard about George Gershwin: one day he suddenly found his fingers stumbling over an arpeggio he had always played easily; he died shortly afterwards of a brain tumour.

We had been warned that cancer patients often developed secondary tumours: with lung cancer, the secondary sites were often in the brain. An urgent visit to the specialist confirmed that a scan showed two brain tumours, and we knew that the treatment available was very limited. We were looking down a tunnel into the future, and the end began to seem in sight. I prayed that Roy might be spared too much suffering, but even in my anguish I felt that God had not deserted us. I was sure he was telling us, 'It isn't finished yet.' He still had work for both of us to do.

Roy had been trying to raise funds for cancer research, and had planned a train journey around the country, called the Tour of Hope. Shortly before it was due to start, Roy was once again having increasing trouble in swallowing, difficulty in breathing, and generally feeling very unwell. Investigations showed that there was no tumour in Roy's oesophagus, but that the tumour on his lung was pressing on his gullet, giving him a sensation that there was always a lump just below his throat. The cancer was so advanced by this stage that all the doctors could do was to try to make him more comfortable, so they increased the dose of morphine to allow him to rest while they completed their tests. That evening I drove him to London where he performed in cabaret!

Soon afterwards, though, his breathing difficulties increased, and he was admitted to hospital again. One evening at around 9 p.m. the specialist rang me at home. He said that Roy had been telling him, with great enthusiasm, about the Tour of Hope. I was absolutely amazed. I hadn't dared to mention the idea to the doctors in case they laughed at me: it was so obvious that Roy was a very sick man, not one who was about to undertake a gruelling fund-raising tour!

'Really?' I answered hesitantly. 'I didn't think he'd be well enough to do it. I've advised the fund-raisers to make contingency plans – it looks as though we'll have to cancel the whole thing.'

'Don't dismiss the idea,' the specialist replied. 'We have ways of patching people up well enough to let them have their final request – only I have to say that it's usually a world cruise, not a train trip round England! I think you'll find we can make him comfortable enough to try it, at least. It seems to mean a lot to him.'

'It does,' I replied. 'He does so hate to let people down.'

When I visited Roy in hospital the next day he was still keen to go on with the tour, in spite of the fact that the heavy sedative he had been given was still making him sound slightly drunk. We went for a mad walk around the hospital grounds together, with Roy walking sideways like a crab, and both of us giggling helplessly at the funny sight we must be.

It wasn't really a laughing matter, of course: Roy needed large doses of morphine to control his pain, and sometimes these made him confused and his speech slurred. The nurses had warned me that already they had been trying to keep the press away, and we knew that when Roy left the hospital they would be there with cameras at the hospital door. I wanted to protect him from this sort of intrusion, but at the same time we wanted to be as open as we could about all aspects of his illness. In the end I went outside first and spoke to the assembled reporters.

'Look,' I said, 'I'm taking Roy home now. Why don't you all go home to our house and wait in the drive? Then we can get home and Roy can settle in, and then you can have your interviews.'

They did as I asked, and we went home quietly. Then Roy sat in a chair and gave the interviews as we had planned. I had warned the reporters that he had had a large dose of morphine, because I didn't want anyone to ridicule his slow, slurred speech, but I need not have worried: as always, Roy responded to the cameras and gave a competent performance.

When he was asked why he was raising funds for something that would obviously come to fruition too late to benefit himself, he replied that there were 40,000 people in Great Britain suffering from lung cancer. 'It's as if I'm pulling on a rope, and there are all those 40,000 behind me pulling too. We want to find a cure for this disease, so I can't let them down. I have to say, "All right back there, chaps?" and we go on pulling together.'

The tour began at Euston, where Roy met all the requests of the photographers, posing by the train that would take us north, and even blowing a guard's whistle and waving a green flag. There was another exhausting round of interviews, and at one point he came very close to passing out. I was all prepared and was supposed to administer the next dose of morphine, but didn't dare give it to him in case he started talking rubbish. From then on we decided that he would give one major interview with all the press present at once, to save his energy.

By now Roy was so ill that he was not strong enough to walk the length of the train to our sleeping compartment, but just rested in an ordinary seat. I was tremendously relieved to meet Pauline Murphy, the specialist cancer nurse who was joining us for the trip. She would be able to give Roy the medication he needed, and to assess the situation and tell us whenever he was doing too much.

We spent that night in Liverpool, where we were given the most tremendous welcome. Many show-business friends were performing in a variety show at the Liverpool Empire called 'For the Love of Roy' in aid of lung cancer research, and Cliff Richard spoke movingly in a televised interview about Roy's faith and his dedication to helping other people. Roy was not well enough to perform, but at the end he walked with help to the middle of the stage, where he received a standing ovation that had to be seen to be believed. As it died down he said, with typical humour, 'Is that all?' Later on he commented, 'I used not to get that much applause after I'd worked my guts out for an hour in cabaret. Now I get it for just making it to the centre of the stage!'

The next day we travelled to Manchester and then Huddersfield, specially chosen because it was Roy's birthplace and an area for which he had tremendous affection and wonderful memories. I woke him up a few times as we were driving across the moors: the views were magnificent and I was aware that this might be his last glimpse of his beloved Yorkshire. He was glad to be woken and mouthed the word 'home' with a warm smile.

His health continued to deteriorate that day: by the time we arrived in Newcastle his face was flushed with fever and he began being sick into a bucket. Simon Bates had volunteered to join us on the trip so that he could help with just such occasions as this; he was already out among the crowds telling them to gather round the coach and that Roy would come to the door to speak to them. There was nothing else to be done, so in my sternest voice I told Roy to stop being sick, pull himself together and get to the door because people were waiting for him, and he did just that!

We went on to Glasgow by air, cutting down our travelling time considerably, but that night in the hotel I was really afraid that he was going to die. Even Pauline, our nurse, admitted that she wasn't sure that he was going to make it. Somehow we were all being fuelled by Roy's indomitable courage and his determination to do something tremendous to raise funds for other sufferers.

I sat in the sitting room of our suite (all the accommodation had been donated by well-wishers to enable the trip to happen) and prayed. A whole series of concerns were buzzing around in my head. I was aware that the whole journey was probably hastening Roy's death, and that I was contributing by going along with it. I was worried that the trip would degrade Roy, by allowing him to appear either stupid, because of the drugs, or ill and seeming to call for pity. And I wondered whether people would get the wrong idea, and think that the trip was being undertaken from the wrong motives – for self-aggrandisement and publicity for its own sake, rather than the publicity desperately needed for fund-raising in a good cause.

I can remember staring out of the window at the twinkling lights of the city, and thinking what a bleak place the world looked. Roy was going through terrible pain, and I was powerless to help him. My mind was racing, trying to decide whether we should abandon the whole plan and fly home where he could get treatment.

'Are we wrong to do this, Jesus?' I prayed. ' Should I persuade Roy to give up and go home? What should I do?'

As I prayed I felt peace steal into my heart. Words from the Bible came into my mind so clearly that I knew God was speaking to me through them: 'Greater love hath no man than this, that he lay down his life for his friends.' Of course! Roy himself would get no benefit from this – his concern was that other people would have a better chance of treatment and recovery. I was able to relax, and trust in God's fatherly love for us, and in his purposes. I was filled with admiration for Roy's spirit in taking on this trip, and I was sure that it was God's will that he would get through it – somehow.

The next morning Roy sat up in bed and said, 'OK, let's get going!' and on we went. Simon Bates said in a TV interview at the time that he personally was finding it increasingly difficult to cope with what was going on. Time after time he saw Roy absolutely exhausted – the drugs drained him of energy – yet whenever there was a show to watch, a child to thank, a group of people who had come to see him, he would make a supreme effort of will and summon up the energy from somewhere to shake hands, crack a joke, and let people know how much he appreciated their efforts to help. Simon himself was wonderful – he always knew just how to command attention in the nicest way, and kept everybody organised.

On Friday we visited Bristol, Plymouth and Cardiff before returning to Waterloo, where we were met by a crowd of friends and well-wishers. Even the porters who carried our bags off the train reached into their pockets and put handfuls of change into the collecting buckets.

We had visited eight cities in four days. It was a punishing schedule by anyone's standards: for a sick man it was ridiculous. Yet at every stop Roy managed to leave the train, even if he had to sit in a wheelchair to move a few yards down the platform. And the money poured in. By the time we reached London it was clear that Roy had raised over a million pounds. He was weak and in pain, and we were both exhausted, but elated because we had succeeded in what we had set out to do. Roy had not only helped the cause of cancer research, he had also cheered and encouraged countless other cancer sufferers.

Three days later he went into hospital for an operation to help his eating difficulty: the surgeon inserted a rigid tube into his oesophagus, so that the tumour could not compress it. The operation left him weaker than ever, and the specialist warned me that Roy might not last the night. Julia was still working in Peru, but I called the rest of the children together. They all arrived at the hospital around 5 p.m. and stood around the bed, uncertain of what they should do; Roy seemed to be unconscious. Daniel took Roy's hand and said softly, 'I love you, Dad,' and burst into tears. That finished us all off, and we all turned away, crying quietly. Suddenly a gruff voice said, 'What's the matter with you all?' and made us all jump. Roy had opened his eyes onto the classic death-bed scene, and as usual played it for a laugh. Once again, against all expectation, he rallied and made some sort of recovery. He wasn't ready to die yet: he would be coming home.

An extract from my diary for July 29th:

After fitful, uncomfortable and exhausted sleep I woke very early about 4.45 and made myself a drink in the staff kitchen at the hospital. I sat drinking it and praying the Lord's Prayer. Then Roy woke. I gave him a drink and wished him a happy 31st Wedding Anniversary, and thanked him for all the years of joy and happiness and love he had given me. I didn't have a card or a present for him, but a heart which over all the years had been and always would be his.

I opened the window wide to allow the fresh morning air to fill the room. The stillness and beauty of the hospital gardens gave me such peace . . . I prayed for my family. I released them once again to God. I relinquished my right once again to everything. All that is in God's hands. I put on, on behalf of us all, God's armour to stand against the enemy's invasion. The helmet of salvation; the breastplate of righteousness – His righteousness; the strong belt of truth – His truth; shoes to speed me on to preach the Gospel of peace, by living it rather than by shouting it.

This reminded me of a letter we had received which told us to show the world 'how a Christian should die'. It had not troubled me but posed questions in my mind: what did this man want us to do? Go through a performance of dying to satisfy his desires? No, I saw that in living and in dying we are Christ's, and what man perceives is not our problem. Alleluia for the release of that responsibility. God was not placing that burden on us . . .

The birds were now singing and finding their breakfasts on the lawn . . . everything has its season, God's perfection for us, His timing in our lives. His numbering of our days, nothing to fear, nothing to weep for. Just pure joy in my heart for all the blessings he had so faithfully and so richly given to us through all our days.

During the time Roy was in hospital I often had time to pray and meditate, and I was grateful for the opportunity; I knew that the time of testing was ahead of us. Roy was discharged after five days, and came home to Gerrards Cross: I knew that I was going to be nursing him from now on. He was fully aware that he was dying, and our time together was all the more precious. He was in a great deal of pain, and I would often stay up all night to give him his medication and talk to him when he was wakeful.

Sometimes we both felt very low and weary of the whole business of suffering; at other times we were uplifted by the support of friends and the comfort of the Holy Spirit. On August 5th I wrote in my diary:

On Monday August 1st when Roy came out of hospital he was very low. When we prayed he said that he felt God had abandoned him and he couldn't feel him anywhere. I felt the same and was very despondent because I couldn't give him any reassurance. Later during the week with this question on my mind I started to think that even if I doubted the Lord, I had nowhere else to go but to Him. I know for a certainty that nothing and no one else could meet my needs, or speak truth, or help me, but the Lord. I could hide nowhere. I have been reading the Psalms – many times the psalmist expresses loneliness, abandonment and desperation. I realise in our humanness we are not alone. This gave me such reassurance . . .

August 6th:

During the past couple of days Roy has been seeing 'indescribable bright lights'. He also expressed 'hearing' the song *Because He lives, I can face tomorrow* which gave him real reassurance. Today we had a beautiful time of communion. I was reminded of Romans 8: Nothing can separate us from the love of God. Roy then prayed: 'O God, thank you for the gift of your Son – such grace . . .' It was so moving to hear him pray so fervently when I had thought he was asleep.

August 7th:

Roy had a very bad night – distressed, in pain and vomiting all through the night – the pain was heightened because of the tube, so we didn't get much sleep. By morning he was very weak with irregular breathing and his eyes were rolling backwards occasionally. I really thought that this was it. I dressed quickly and sat with him holding his hand, telling him I loved him. He asked me to kiss him, his voice an almost inaudible whisper. He told me that he had always loved me and that nothing had ever made him change his mind.

After a while a big smile came over his face and he said 'Oh, yes, it's just beautiful, so soft, so warm. The pain – it's still there but it's so comfortable. There's nothing to worry about.'

I was crying, but I would have been so happy had Jesus come for him then. But he gradually started getting stronger and the pain returned . . .

Antonia and Benjamin are both away. Roy had a bad night, and we were whispering together when I suddenly said, 'Why are we whispering? We're alone in the house, we can party!'

'Isn't it amazing?' said Roy. 'If we were Jewish we'd have the whole family wailing at the bedside, but as it is we've been abandoned!'

August 9th:

Sitting at Roy's bedside I saw a smile spreading across his face – this after a night and day of vomiting and great pain. I went over and asked why the smile. He whispered back almost inaudibly. 'It's beautiful . . . the most wonderful gardens. What a gardener! I thought I was a gardener, but this gardener's something else.' I asked him if the pain was gone and he said, no, but about half of it was gone. 'It's so lovely – don't hang about, darling! I don't know that I'm going to die yet, but I've got to be patient.'

As the days wore on, Roy's pain became more intense, and the dose of morphine he was taking had to be raised. In the end the doctor fitted him with a syringe 'driver' which administers a regular dose of the medication every two minutes, and can be boosted whenever necessary. Towards the end of the month Rob and Di Parsons came for a visit, and they could see clearly the change in Roy, especially in his decreasing awareness. At times he was perfectly lucid, but much of the time he was sleepy, or in a world of his own when he could not really respond to conversation.

I still could not decide whether to tell Julia to come home – so often Roy had seemed on the brink of death, only to rally once more. Roy was well enough to speak to her on the phone himself, and he told her, 'If you want to come home for your own benefit, then come. If you're thinking of coming because of me, don't – I don't want to disrupt your life.' Julia thanked him, went to the travel agent, and took the first flight home.

By the time she arrived Roy was scarcely able to speak, but he was able to recognise her, for which I was profoundly grateful. He even remembered where she had been: for the first day, every time she came into the room he would smile broadly and whisper, 'Julia! Peru!'

Julia later wrote about that journey home:

I wasn't sure what to expect when I got there: I imagined someone coming to the airport and saying I was too late – that he'd already died. That would have been awful – he would have thought I didn't care. Dan and Birthe picked me up from the airport and started explaining Dad's condition. It made me cry. It was difficult to imagine him not being in control.

It was such a relief when I got home and he recognised me, but it was very hard, seeing him in that state: the others had been watching a gradual deterioration, but for me it was a real shock. He could still make us all laugh, though: when I walked into the room for the first time, he was so surprised to see me that he tried to get out of bed. We asked him what he was doing and he said he was going to the gobsmackler shop!

I had been so busy in Peru that I hadn't realised how important for my own peace of mind it was for me to be there. At one point Dad looked round at us all and said, 'Oh – we were waiting for someone, weren't we. We don't have to wait any more.' That meant a lot to me, as it showed he knew I was there.

Those last few days were very difficult, and I was glad to have the family around us. For his birthday on 31st August we had made an ice-cream cake – the only thing that would slip down his throat. When we sang Happy Birthday he smiled and whispered 'Happy Birthday', and seemed to know what was happening. There had been many tributes to him in the media, and we took a radio into his room for the Gloria Hunniford Show: she played *Good Morning* from the show *Singing in the Rain*, a song which Roy and Tommy Steele had danced to. Roy followed it very carefully, as if remembering the steps, and when it was over he said thoughtfully, 'That was very difficult.' They were his last real words.

On the last night I sat up beside him as his breathing grew shallower and his pulse weaker, and I knew that at last the battle was over. I didn't want to disturb the children, so I lay down on the bed beside him and held his hand, and felt his spirit slip away. He died at 5.15 on the morning of Friday 2nd September, free at last of pain and suffering, and went home to the Lord Jesus whom he had loved and followed for so long.

6
Saying Goodbye

Strangely, on the morning that Roy died I had the distinct impression that his spirit had left his body about an hour before he finally stopped breathing. I was tired after my many nights of nursing and yet I felt quite calm. I had been expecting this for so long, and my overwhelming feeling was relief that his suffering was over. I lay beside him for a few moments longer, and then I got up and opened the curtains. It was almost dawn, and the sky was growing lighter, but I felt it was still too early to wake the family. I went downstairs and made myself a pot of tea, then I came back to look after Roy for the last time.

I washed him and tidied the bed, and packed away the syringe driver that had delivered the morphine. Then I thought, I'm going to have a busy day today, so I went and washed my hair.

It seems odd to me now, but I suppose I was operating on a sort of auto-pilot in which my practical nature took over and suggested the next activity. It seems to be a common reaction – I remember a neighbour telephoning me to tell me that her husband had died; I rushed round at once, to find her putting on her make-up and doing her hair. Her comment was, 'Well, the doctor will be here in a minute!'

At about seven o'clock I made more drinks and took trays up to the bedrooms, woke the children and told them that Roy had died. They all came in to our bedroom and we prayed together round the bed. No one was sobbing aloud, but we were all very emotional and weepy.

Then I turned to Benjamin and said, 'What are you going to do about Blackpool?'

It was the day when the Blackpool illuminations were to be switched on: Shirley Bassey was going to throw the switch, and then hand over a cheque for cancer research. Ben was planning to be there anyway, with the National Youth Jazz Orchestra, and he was supposed to receive the cheque on Roy's behalf. If he went, he would have to leave the house at 9 a.m.

'Why don't you go and pray about it for a while?' I suggested. Ben hesitated for a moment, and then said, almost at once, 'I'll go. I know Dad would want me to.'

I was very proud of him. He told me later that when he got on the coach which was taking the orchestra to Blackpool, he told everyone at once that Roy had died. He thought it would be easier than to have each one in turn asking him how his father was. In fact, the whole group were immensely supportive: by the time they arrived in Blackpool the news of Roy's death had broken, and outside the place where they were playing a newspaper hoarding bore the words 'Roy Castle is dead'. Two of his friends tore the paper off the sign – a kind act of vandal-ism as they didn't want Ben to see such a stark statement.

Meanwhile, back in Gerrards Cross, I decided that the next job was to find an undertaker. The husband of our church caretaker had died fairly recently, so I knew that she would know how to go about it. I went down to the church to see her. I was fine until I started telling her why I had come, but then I broke down and cried as she hugged me. Graham Dawson, one of the pastors of our church, was leading a men's morning prayer meeting. He offered to contact the undertaker for me, so I went home and started on my list of people to ring. At the top was our doctor, of course, and he promised to come to the house at about 10 a.m. after his surgery and write the death certificate.

Telling other people was a delicate matter: I had to keep saying to them, 'Please keep this quiet until I've had a chance to contact all the family,' because I wanted to tell them myself, and not have them find out at second hand through the media. As usual, I was wary of the press finding out too soon; once they knew, everything would become public, so I knew I had to be careful and organ-ised in what I did. Even the undertaker was told to come 'in an unmarked van' – like a spy! – so that no one would find out by accident.

I was still at the phone, working through my list, at lunchtime. Inevitably, though, there was a slip: I rang one show-business friend who happened to speak to his agent five minutes later; the agent contacted a reporter and the story was out. I was irritated because I hadn't yet managed to track down my sister, and she heard of Roy's death from someone else – exactly the situation I had been trying so hard to avoid.

One person who had been near the top of my list was Roy's agent, and of course the reporters descended on him as soon as they knew. He rang me to warn me that the press were on their way, and said that they were bound to want a statement from me. I said the first thing that came into my head: 'No flowers, no fuss, no mourning, just lots of joy.' 'That's great,' he replied, 'that'll do,' and he put down the phone. Ten minutes later the newsreader on ITN's lunchtime news announced Roy's death and repeated the words I had said.

Half an hour later two TV crews arrived at the house, from Carlton and Sky News. I told them to set up their equipment on the patio and I would come out and see them. Alison Jack, the presenter, had brought me a beautiful bouquet of flowers; she had interviewed us several times during Roy's illness, and she was clearly upset at having to intrude on us at this time. I felt very sorry for her, being put in such an awkward position, and I wanted to make them all feel more comfortable about it. So I gave the interviews and was as normal as possible, and managed to make them laugh and relax. Then I got the giggles, because I didn't seem to be behaving much like a grieving widow, worrying about whether I'd made enough coffee for an army of cameramen and trying to cheer everyone up.

After the television crews came the newspaper reporters, so I took them into the sitting room out of the way. At about one o'clock the undertaker came (in his plain van as arranged) to take away Roy's body. Daniel came into the room, closing the door behind him, and raised his eyebrows meaningfully at me: there was a tremendous banging and bumping as the coffin was manoeuvred with difficulty round the narrow turn in the stairs. I was desperately speaking more and more loudly over the top of all this, and trying to keep them all talking until the coast was clear – I did *not* want pictures of Roy's coffin in the papers.

The phone was ringing constantly, and I was very glad that my first instinct had been to request no flowers, or doubtless there would have been a traffic jam of florist's vans too. It wasn't that I didn't appreciate people's love and concern – I was very grateful for it – but the sheer scale of the response was simply very difficult for us to deal with. At about four p.m. I went with my sisters Liza and Mauny to Beaconsfield, to register Roy's death. It was the first quiet moment I had had all day.

It may seem odd that our activities were dominated by the press in this way, but it didn't occur to any of us to shut the door and tell them to go away and leave us to grieve in private. This was not because we wanted publicity: neither Roy nor I had ever sought publicity, even when Roy was working on the stage and on television. All he ever wanted was to do his job as well as he could: that brought him all the work he needed. But inevitably that work brought him into the public eye, and so we were used to seeing his picture in the newspaper and on TV. The press were almost as much a part of our everyday experience of life as the milkman.

Once his cancer was diagnosed and it became known

that he was fighting the disease Roy had developed a new role, cheering and encouraging his many fellow-sufferers. Many patients and their carers wrote to tell us how much it helped to see Roy facing treatments and the side effects of treatment (such as his baldness) with such courage and good humour, and how thrilled they were to receive a postcard or a phone call from him to cheer them on. Only his role as a public figure enabled him to do this – a strange kind of power but a real one in our modern world.

Additionally, once Roy became involved with fund-raising, he realised that publicity was a lifeline for charities. That was the reason for the endless photo-calls and interviews and the tremendous railway tour which visited so many cities. The aim was to touch as many people's lives as possible, to raise everyone's awareness of the disease and the need for research to beat it, and to collect the much-needed money for funding. We knew that the press were invaluable allies in enabling this to happen.

Finally, although we never tried to manipulate situations, we were always honest with anyone who interviewed us about our Christian faith and our allegiance to the Lord Jesus Christ. We never grabbed anyone by the collar and asked them if they were saved! But we always took every opportunity to show that we were ordinary Christians, doing our best to follow Jesus, and living out our lives in the way we believed he wanted us to.

This was why when Roy died I carried on just as we had always lived, accepting the role of the press as part of our life, and giving interviews and photographs as a kind of due, a repayment to the public for all the support and affection they had shown our family over the years and especially during the last few months of Roy's illness.

In fact I scarcely had time to analyse my own feelings on that first day when Roy died. I had been busy all day, and I had to remain calm to give interviews and to allow the TV crews the shots they wanted for filming, walking down the garden and holding photos of Roy. My over-whelming sensation was one of relief that Roy was no longer in pain; because we had been prepared for his death for so long, it did not come as so much of a shock. Grief was not a new experience into which I had been thrust suddenly, because I think I had been grieving for him for a long time already.

I was very tired, though, and I didn't feel at all hungry. Julia kept following me round the house with tasty morsels trying to tempt me to eat something, but all I could manage were little pieces of bread, and hot milk and honey. Julia was worried, too, that I wouldn't be able to sleep, and even went to the chemist and asked for a mild sleeping pill to help me. In fact I was exhausted and slept deeply that night when the house was finally quiet. The sleeping tablet was redundant, and remained that way.

The next day Jim Graham, our pastor, came back from Ireland where he had been attending a conference, and came to see us. I asked him if I could speak at a service at church one Sunday, to thank everyone for all their prayers for Roy. He said, 'Yes, whenever you're ready.' I replied, 'I'm ready now,' so we arranged it for the next day. I knew that many of our friends had gone on praying for Roy's healing, long after all hope – in earthly terms – had gone. I wanted to thank them for that, but I didn't want them to be bewildered by Roy's dying. I wanted them all to know that Roy had died on God's appointed day.

On Sunday I walked to church early to pray with Jim and to sort out some arrangements, only to find, to my horror, a camera team from Carlton Television waiting. I nearly changed my mind about the whole thing: I was very much afraid that people might think that by offering to stand up and speak in church I was pushing myself into the limelight, and that it had been set up. In the end I went through with it. After all, I reasoned, if it was the right thing to do without the press there, it was no less right just because they had turned up unexpectedly. I really couldn't keep worrying about what people might think. It was harder to talk to all our friends at church with the cameras there, but I managed it, and thanked them for all their love and support.

In many ways the constant attention of the press was a help – it kept me focused on what was important. All the interviews asked basic questions about how Roy would be remembered, how he had faced death, and how I was coping with bereavement. Over and over again I was able to tell people of the great Christian expectation, and that Roy had not feared death because he knew where he was going, to be with the Lord Jesus. Although he had grown weary of the pain and suffering on the path to death, he had never lost his sense of humour, and even in the last days he was smiling and saying 'Happy Birthday' to himself. I was secure in knowing that he was now free of pain, and I trusted Jesus to look after him for me, so although I missed him dreadfully, I could only rejoice in his release from his body.

One major job in those first days was dealing with the mail: we received at least one sack each day for the first week, and we hardly had time even to open all those envelopes. However, I was determined that every letter should have a reply of some sort, and a student friend came in to help. We divided them into three piles: those from total strangers received a formal note thanking them for their messages; those from people who had written a more personal letter received a typed letter to which I added a handwritten postscript; and I wrote personal letters to all our friends. Just addressing all the envelopes was a major burden on top of all the other activities, but it was wonderful to hear from so many people who had cared for Roy over so many years, and I was so grateful for such love and support.

The most urgent task was to make plans for the thanksgiving service, and I was determined to make time to do that properly. I gathered the family together, and we put 'Do not disturb' signs on the front and back doors and took the phone off the hook. I was not sure quite how we would manage, but we prayed together for guidance, and then we each offered our ideas. I wanted a simple, homespun service, which would honour God and pay tribute to Roy, for all the local people, the neighbours and shopkeepers who had known him for years. It all fell into place with great harmony, and when Jim arrived to join the discussion he accepted all our suggestions happily. One fear was that the church would be under siege from the press and people wanting to watch, and our quiet funeral for family and church friends would become a spectacle. Whenever I had spoken to friends who lived a long way away I had put them off from coming to the service, by promising that we would hold a public memorial service in London in the near future, somewhere that would hold a large number of people, and more easily accessible than Gerrards Cross.

After I had given that first interview to Sky TV on Friday morning after Roy died, they had asked if I would let them film the service. I really didn't want anything to intrude on the service, and I certainly didn't want it to turn into a production, but I said that if the church office agreed, they could put in one camera. In fact it quickly became clear that allowing Sky to film would be a help: there would be only one camera team in church (and they promised to be unobtrusive), and they would allow the rest of the television news services to pick up the pictures from their base in Croydon. They also helped by setting up sound systems and closed-circuit TV screens in the church hall and outside the church, so that all the over-spill crowds could still take part.

Harry Secombe was away on holiday. I rang him in Majorca to tell him what was planned, but I told him not to worry about coming home. 'It's all right,' he replied. 'Myra's had our bags packed since last Wednesday!' The funeral would be on the afternoon of Thursday, 8th September; it was Harry's birthday.

Roy's body was cremated in the morning, at a separate event at the crematorium. We didn't tell anyone that there would be no coffin at the service in church, because we wanted the morning to be completely private for the immediate family. We worked very hard at this, arranging for the hearse to come to the crematorium alone, and making our own way there separately in our own cars, so there was no 'procession' to follow. This was our 'time to weep'. Fortunately this time most of the press did not find out what was happening; two reporters did turn up, but we asked them to leave and they did so – though I confess I kept looking towards the bushes to make sure no more were lurking anywhere! The service at the crematorium was short and simple, led lovingly by our own pastor, Jim Graham. The only decoration was a large spray of autumn flowers and leaves in golds and browns, which looked like a warm splash of golden sunshine.

I think it was the bleakest moment of my life when I watched the hearse come up the drive to the crematorium. We were all gathered in the ante-room, and as I looked out of the window at the coffin being lifted, the subdued chatter of the others made me want to scream, 'Can't you all be quiet? That's my husband in there.' Any kind of conversation was intolerable to me just then. Julia cried and Anne Graham comforted her, but I didn't dare cry: I knew that if I let go then I would be unable to stop.

Roy's ashes were scattered. I didn't want them put in a special place or on to a special flower bed; once his spirit had gone, his body was not important to me, because it wasn't him any more. I can understand that some people wish to cherish even those remains, and this is part of their way of working through their grief. A good friend of mine, for instance, scattered the ashes of her husband in places they loved, where they had been happy together.

Some people keep the ashes in a jar on the shelf! I simply didn't feel the need for this and decided that it wasn't worth making a fuss about it.

After the cremation we went home for lunch; more friends had arrived for the afternoon funeral service – Cliff Richard, Joan Morecambe (Eric's widow) and her daughter Gail and granddaughter Amelia (who is my god-daughter), Rob Parsons and others. We had arranged a simple Ploughman's Lunch, but even that is complicated to serve to thirty-five people. In the middle of it all, as we were rushing around, Julia said in exasperation, 'Oh, where's Dad?!' I knew what she meant – he was always good at jollying things along, and we could just have done with his help!

Harry Secombe was very emotional: as it was his birthday I had bought him a silly present, a sort of toy duck, and he didn't know whether to laugh or cry. A funeral lunch party is incredibly difficult to host, as people are afraid to be happy.

At the church there were crowds of people, and it was difficult to see and greet everyone. A TV screen had been placed outside the church for those who couldn't get inside; it was a blustery day with the odd shower, but still a crowd stood there throughout the service. I don't think anyone got too wet.

The day before we had received a most inspired gift from a friend, the manager of a nearby hotel where Roy and I sometimes swam. It was a huge bouquet of helium balloons covered with clowns and stars: we took them to the church and placed them at one side, where they bobbed and floated: an ideal remembrance of Roy's impish humour. On the other side was a large blown-up picture of Roy.

Daniel, Anto and Ben played in the church orchestra, and Julia read from Psalm 112. Harry Secombe spoke about Roy the entertainer: 'He was the best of us . . . he had more talent than the rest of us . . . he could sing, he could dance, he could act, he could write, he could play lots of instruments – and if he'd taken up embroidery, he'd have been a record-breaker at that, too!' Rob Parsons spoke about Roy the family man, and the joy he found in our marriage and in the four children. Daniel spoke of Roy the father, and his wife Birthe read from Exodus 34, verses 6 and 7: 'The Lord, the Lord, the compassionate and gracious God, slow to anger, abounding in love and faithfulness, maintaining love to thousands, and forgiving wickedness, rebellion and sin.' Ray Donnelly described Roy working tirelessly for the Lung Cancer Fund, and told how he had watched Roy visiting a cancer ward and speaking to every patient with a smile and joke and a special word, even though he was at the time very ill himself. Anto read from Living Light, and Les Moir spoke about Roy's last music recording session, making a jazz praise album with Benjamin. I told everyone about Roy's birthday, which was the last day he was really conscious: he had suddenly raised both his arms and said, 'Jesus Christ is my Saviour! Jesus Christ is my Lord! – Hey Jesus!' Carl McGregor sang a wonderful song, which spoke so well of the family's feelings, and got the whole congregation dancing:

> He's turned my mourning into dancing again
> He's lifted my sorrow

I can't stay silent
I must sing for his joy has come.

Where there once was only hurt
He gave his healing hand
Where there once was only pain
He brought comfort like a friend.

All in all it was a joyful occasion: we remembered Roy and we laughed and sang his favourite hymns – all good jazzy arrangements! – in the building where he had worshipped for seventeen years.

After the service we went back to the house for a cup of tea. It seemed to be a very long one – after an hour and a half there were still fifty people in the house! At the end of the day, after everyone had gone, Jim Graham came to pray with us, which helped us a great deal. At the funeral he had reminded us of Roy's words: 'The day of my funeral – that will be my finest performance!'

Over the last few months of Roy's illness, we had realised that he was going to die. Mostly I was so busy, just getting through each day, that I didn't have much time to worry about the future or how I would cope after he was dead. After his death there were times – especially at night – when I felt anxious and lonely, but mostly I just kept going. Every day was still so busy, getting things organised and carrying on with those parts of Roy's work which I could do – speaking about cancer research, for instance – that I had no time to feel sorry for myself.

Sometimes I was tempted to feel that Roy's death was, in the words of the Graham Kendrick song, 'the failure of my plans'. He had not been healed, there was no triumph: and then I would always realise that God's purposes were being worked out, not our earthly plans and desires. God had taken Roy to himself in his own time, and Roy had touched many lives before he died.

I wasn't always able to be confident and positive. Two weeks after the funeral I was asked to appear on a new programme about faith, to be broadcast on Sunday mornings. Sue Cook was interviewing me and being very sweet and helpful, but the recording didn't go smoothly. Several parts had to be done two or three times and I began to get muddled: I couldn't remember whether or not I was repeating myself. I felt very inadequate and was sure I was making a mess of it. In addition, it was the first time since Roy had died that I had been to London on my own. Suddenly just the effort of getting myself around seemed exhausting and threatening, and I felt very vulnerable.

I realise now that it was still very soon after Roy's death, and I was still reeling from all the events of the previous six months. I knew that I was capable of carrying on and running my own life, but I felt raw and bruised and tearful. It was a very low moment.

One of the hardest things to deal with was being told by other people how I should be feeling. Of course I had some bad times, but according to some people, I didn't have nearly enough of them! Many otherwise kind people seemed to take a pleasure in being directive about responses to grief: 'You will be feeling dreadful,' they said, and seemed to sit back and watch for it. That first Christmas we had so many deeply gloomy cards predicting our misery ('We know how sad you will be at Christmas . . . you will miss Roy more than ever') that it became a family joke. As we opened our presents or started carving the turkey Ben would ask, 'Are we having a terrible time yet?' In fact we had a lovely Christmas, just as Roy would have wanted us to. We laughed a lot and cried a little, and remembered him all the time with love and joy.

It wasn't necessarily the anniversaries or special days which were difficult, but little things: finding a letter, seeing an item of clothing, catching sight of someone in a crowded street who walks the same way as Roy . . . Mostly I just got on with life, like everyone else. The difficulty was that if I was normal and happy, people suggested that I hadn't yet come through to reality, and that sooner or later I would crack up and succumb to grief. I was perfectly willing to accept that this might be the case – I didn't pretend to know everything that would happen – but in all the years since his death the breakdown never seemed to arrive. I know that Roy is with Jesus and that gives me great peace. I am greatly blessed by a loving family and friends, and I know that as I commit every day to the Lord, I am walking in his will. I am sorry if my joy offends anyone, but I cannot be less than honest about who I am and what I feel, because I can only ever be honest with God, the Father who knows all our hearts. 'The dreams of all I hope to be, The truth of what I am.' After all, that is why Jesus came, to release us from all our posturing and pretences into his glorious love and light, to be truly ourselves.

7
Sunshine and Shadow

I have never been a great weeper. This is partly because I was brought up to be 'sensible': our wartime generation were taught that it was admirable to be brave and to endure. The boarding school I attended disapproved of any display of emotion, so I quickly learned to suppress my feelings. I could weep easily on stage or when I was watching films, but I hardly ever cried during my own personal crises. However, tears can be very therapeutic, and I have certainly discovered the release of crying over the past few years.

When Roy was first diagnosed with lung cancer, the shock brought tears with it for the first twenty-four hours or so, while my mind and emotions adjusted to the possibilities ahead of us. It was when we told Ben about Roy, and I watched him struggling to keep his composure, that I realised how important it was that we should be free to express how we were feeling. So often we repress our tears in order not to embarrass other people, but within the family we had to be able to be ourselves, to support one another and to give each other permission to be sad.

Outside the family, though, I understand how awkward it makes people feel to see others crying; friends feel helpless in the face of the open expression of grief which they cannot cure. So I developed a way of 'diverting' my tears at inopportune times, and determinedly thinking about something else to drive the tears away. After a few weeks I realised that I was getting headaches, and occasionally taking aspirin to relieve them – something I usually try not to do. I soon realised that all I needed to do was to allow the tears to flow, and then the headaches disappeared: crying was a way of releasing the stress of pent-up emotions, and had a healing and calming effect.

For many years Roy worked on the *Record Breakers* programme on Children's BBC, presenting other people's record-breaking attempts and achieving quite a few himself. After his death, the next series started by devoting the first programme to all Roy's records, as a tribute to him. It showed clips of all his daring exploits over the years: parascending under the bridges on the Thames, wing-walking on a plane flying to France across the channel, and tap-dancing his way into the record books. It was a very moving tribute, and I sat and watched it on TV with Julia and Benj. Cheryl Baker had been Roy's colleague and co-presenter on the programme, and as the last clip ended she was supposed to turn professionally to the camera and speak the lines from the script. Instead, with tears pouring down her face, she said, 'I'm sorry, Roy,' and put her head in her hands. Just as we were watching this the phone rang: we all looked at each other and said together, 'I can't answer it', because we were all crying. When I did blow my nose and answer the phone, it was a friend who had been watching the show and who was also in floods of tears.

Nowadays the tears come to me much more easily. One occasion when I found it very hard to control my feelings was when I was being photographed in a room full of huge photos of Roy. While the others were busy setting up the cameras I looked around at all the pictures of my husband, and on an impulse I privately kissed the tip of my finger and touched it to his face. In an instant my eyes filled up with tears and I had to smother myself in a large tissue very quickly – I'm sure the photos they took of me must have been rather pink and blotchy ones!

I tried hard not to become emotional in public, though; I tried to be aware of other people's feelings, and I knew that often they were scared about how I would react if they talked about Roy. The tone was set by that first Sky interview, when Alison, the interviewer, was obviously nervous about having to approach me a few hours after Roy's death. I was so keen to reassure her that I decided I had to be very normal and relaxed.

The same approach worked well when I went to the local shops: I went with a smile and talked to people, and then they didn't feel they had to avoid me. Often people who have been bereaved are made to feel even more isolated because friends who don't know what to say dare not telephone or visit them. I jumped right in and chatted to people, so their difficulty disappeared. The morning after Roy's funeral service I went to Pop-In, the Mums and

Toddlers Group organised by our church, to make the tea and coffee as usual; otherwise the mums and the other helpers might have been wondering how I was going to react. I went in and spoke about Roy and behaved as normally as possible – I thought it was best to get on with life straight away, and let them see that life goes on.

These experiences have affected me in other ways, too. I think that I have become much more sensitive to other people's grief, because I have been through it myself. Bereavement seems to open up the emotions. All deaths seem more immediate, more vivid to me now, because I have seen it so close at hand, and I feel I can more truly share in the sorrow of other people.

At the same time I know that all deaths are part of the great cycle of life: the leaves fall to feed the soil, the seeds die to germinate again, and our earthly bodies die while our spirits go on to heavenly life. If we stand on God's side of it we know there is an eternal pattern and purpose to everything that happens, and this can help us to endure our own pain. But that intellectual knowledge, though it helps us to understand and explain, does not enable us to stand outside our own emotions, and it does not allow us to escape from or deny the pain of our loss.

There is no way out of grief but through it. There is no magic formula, no spiritual or emotional trick which can let us off the hook. The passage of time may eventually enable us to get used to the feeling of being alone, but not even that will change the fact of our bereavement. The Holy Spirit will bring us comfort and peace, but God will not protect us from the reality of what it is to be human:

he wants our eyes to be open to that reality, and fixed upon Jesus. He knew the greatest pain it is possible for mankind to know – injustice, desolation, desertion and a cruel and painful death. He knows and shares our grief, and he shows us how to face it: not with bitterness or anger, but with love and gentleness. If we fix our eyes upon him, we can find a way through our distress.

We cannot escape from grief, but we can choose how we go through it. We can allow ourselves to be defeated by grief, or we can survive it. I am not suggesting a false cheerfulness which only puts a mask over our feelings: that would be dishonest to ourselves and to everyone else. But we can apply the considerable power of our will, to decide how we will approach this experience. We can decide whether we will collapse before the cold wind of grief, or whether we will bend in the wind like a young tree, and spring back to grow up towards the sun. As everything we do and everything we see reminds us of our loved one, we can choose either to be swamped with sorrow at every turn, or we can rejoice in the happy memories which come flooding back.

Several people warned me about how difficult it would be to clear out Roy's clothes – but does it have to be? I tried to tackle the job cheerfully; after all, if Roy had been there and decided that he didn't need them, he would gladly have given them away. One day, though, I found a pair of his trousers which had escaped my clearing out, because they were in the washing basket. I washed and ironed them and carried them upstairs to the wardrobe, and then suddenly burst into tears: it hit me all over again that I wouldn't be washing things or caring for him any more.

When Roy worked in cabaret, he was often asked to do special shows for companies. He had a long song with the chorus 'Tooralai, tooralai, tooralai-ay', to which he would make up extra verses. He would get someone in the firm to tell him details of all the well-known characters, the managers, secretaries, directors and foremen, and then he would put on glasses, false teeth or a wig, and imitate them. It always got a tremendous response – but it required an extensive wardrobe of props.

Roy was a hoarder: he kept everything, and he often bought items – a funny hat, a scarf or a wig – when he saw them, 'just in case' they ever came in useful. But when the time came he could never find the item he wanted, and would invariably have to go out and buy another. After he died I started to clear out the room behind the garage he used for rehearsing, and found the most enormous quantity of boxes and bags, full of props, pins, sewing things, hats and so on. It could have been deeply depressing, and I could have mourned over every item he had chosen and used. Instead, as Antonia said, 'Guess who's got the last laugh?' – I had always complained about the amount of stuff Roy hoarded, and now I was the one having to clear it all out. I had to give in and laugh with him!

This important matter of being honest with myself includes being honest about Roy. People often put him on a pedestal because he was well known and because of his bravery and selflessness during his illness. That is all true, and I admire and love him for that. But at the same time he was an ordinary bloke, he wasn't perfect and neither am I, and sometimes he irritated me! This is part of choosing how to face bereavement: I am sad and I miss Roy, but I still view him clearly, as the real person he was.

I don't want him to be canonised by death, because I don't want his memory to be changed from the person I knew. If I were to pretend that he was other than he was, if I were to fantasise and let him become some kind of perfect person in my mind just because he is dead, I would lose him even more thoroughly than I have lost him now. I need the real memories of our real life together, warts and all, to sustain me, not some fairy-tale. Being honest about those things somehow makes them more bearable.

Another aspect of dealing with the sorrow of these 'broken times' is learning how to distinguish between genuine grief and self-pity. There are so many moments, especially in the early days after a death, when grief threatens to overwhelm us. One of the most common for me was the mistaken recognitions – when I would catch sight of someone in a crowd whose back view looked just like Roy's, or who walked in the same way, and my mind, caught unawares, would think, 'There's Roy!' The mistake was only momentary, and then realisation would flood in, but the pain would be intense. This is a natural part of grieving, as the unconscious mind learns to catch up with what the conscious mind knows, and we must allow ourselves to experience this sorrow.

One day, however, I was returning from Scotland, and arrived at Heathrow during a busy rush hour. Lots of people were standing around waiting to meet arrivals, and my eye was caught by a pretty young girl who was anxiously searching the sea of faces in the hall. Then a man approached her, recognition and delight spread across her face, and she threw herself into his arms. I found myself bursting into uncontrollable tears. There was no one to meet me. I had lost that special relationship for ever, and I felt more cold and alone in that moment than I had for a long time.

Then I realised that I was envious of the young couple and their love: love which Roy and I had experienced in our time. I was simply wallowing in self-pity – poor old me, I used to have someone like that, but not any more. It was too much like watching an old movie on television – I could almost hear the orchestra! – and I gave myself a stern talking-to. Grief is natural, and a process we must undergo, but self-pity is unattractive and self-centred. It is important to distinguish between the two.

I think that discerning this difference early on was very helpful to me: I learned to let go with real grief, but to control any impulses towards self-pity. Self-pity tends towards envy of what others may be enjoying, and it centres on some obscure sense that we have been de-prived of something to which we have a right. Whenever I began to feel like this I reminded myself that I have no rights, because my life is not my own. I gave my life to Christ – and I didn't add a postscript, 'and please make it a wonderful life, and protect me from all pain.' There were some very bleak times during the last part of Roy's life when we both felt as if God had abandoned us; we felt no comfort, and no respite from the onslaught. I started to question the reality of my faith and what would happen if I abandoned God. That in itself brought comfort as I realised that there was nowhere else to go, no one in the world I could completely trust. I reminded myself of the transformation Jesus had made in the whole of my life when I discovered this spiritual reality. From there I began to 'enter into his suffering' by knowing a little of what Jesus himself must have felt when he was separated from God on the cross by my sin. Jesus who was sinless cried out to his Father, 'My God, my God, why have you forsaken me?' because sin came between him and God. Jesus was alone then, so what right had I to complain?

Some time ago I came across this beautiful but anonymous meditation.

He had no rights:
No right to a soft bed, and a well-laid table;
No right to a home of his own, a place where his own
    pleasure might be sought;
No right to choose pleasant, congenial companions, those
    who could understand him and sympathise with him;
No right to shrink away from contact with sin, to pull his
    garments closer around him and walk in cleaner paths;
No right to be understood and appreciated; no not by those
    on whom he had poured out a double portion of his love;
No right even never to be forsaken by his Father, the one
    who meant more than all to him.

His only right was to endure shame, spitting, blows; to take
    his place as a sinner at the dock; to bear my sins in
    anguish on the cross.
He had no rights. And I?
A right to the comforts of life? No, but a right to the love of
    God for my pillow.

A right to physical safety? No, but a right to the security of being in his will.

A right to love and sympathy from those around me? No, but a right to the friendship of the one who understands me better than I do myself.

A right to be a leader among men? No, but a right to be led by the one to whom I have given my all, led as a little child, with its hand in the hand of its father.

A right to a home, and dear ones? No, not necessarily; but a right to dwell in the heart of God.

A right to myself? No, but oh, *I have a right to Christ.*

All that he takes I will give;
All that he gives I will take;
He, my only right! He, the one right before which all other rights fade into nothingness.
I have full right to him: Oh, may he have full right to me!

Now when I have any doubts or fears, envy or self-pity, I go back to Psalm 139:

> Where can I go from your Spirit?
> Where can I flee from your presence?
> If I go up to the heavens, you are there;
> If I make my bed in the depths, you are there.
> If I rise on the wings of the dawn,
> if I settle on the far side of the sea,
> even there your hand will guide me,
> your right hand will hold me fast.
>
> If I say, 'Surely the darkness will hide me
> and the light become night around me,'
> even the darkness will not be dark to you;
> the night will shine like the day
> for darkness is as light to you (Psalm 139:7–12).

It reminds me where my real security lies. Who else am I to turn to? I have nothing else to do in my life but follow the Lord. When we follow Jesus we put away all thoughts of rights or personal desires, and fix our eyes only on serving him in his will. Self-pity has no place in a life of service.

Real grief, however, I have to deal with in my own way. If I am busy, I may have to bottle up my emotions for a while – it is my concern and I don't have to inflict it on everyone else – but when I am alone I let go and have a good cry. It's positive, healthy and therapeutic, and I always feel better afterwards. I find it easiest to cry in my prayer-time, when I am talking to the Lord about Roy, or about the things I can't do without him. Sometimes I say to Jesus, 'I am missing him dreadfully – please give him a hug from me.' It's wonderful to have a Father who knows all our feelings and thoughts, so we can be completely honest about them.

> O Lord, you have searched me and you know me.
> You know when I sit and when I rise;
> you perceive my thoughts from afar.
> You discern my going out and my lying down;
> you are familiar with all my ways.
> Before a word is on my tongue
> you know it, Lord (Psalm 139:1–4).

One reason for my determined rejection of anything which smacks of self-pity is that I have indulged in it too much in the past, when I suffered periodic bouts of depression. Although I know that often there is nothing we can do about real clinical depression, nevertheless sometimes I wallowed in it, and now I am very wary of anything which allows me to think too much about 'poor old me'.

I try very hard not to be an object of pity. Sympathy is very welcome and a comfort, but pity has a corrosive effect on our will: we are very easily convinced that our situation is so awful that no effort from us can make it any better. And of course, being in that condition can be very comfortable, in a painful sort of way. After all, if things are really that bad, no one can expect us to do anything: we are relieved of all responsibility.

I am reminded of Jesus' words to the man at the pool of Bethesda: 'Do you want to get well?'

> Now there is in Jerusalem near the Sheep Gate a pool, which in Aramaic is called Bethesda, and which is surrounded by five covered colonnades. Here a great number of disabled people used to lie – the blind, the lame, the paralysed. One who was there had been an invalid for thirty-eight years. When Jesus saw him lying there and learned that he had been in that condition for a long time, he asked him, 'Do you want to get well?'
>
> 'Sir,' the invalid replied, ' I have no one to help me into the pool when the water is stirred. While I am trying to get in, someone else goes down ahead of me.'
>
> Then Jesus said to him, 'Get up! Pick up your mat and walk.' At once the man was cured; he picked up his mat and walked (John 5:2–9).

The story of the pool of Bethesda was that from time to time an angel would come down and stir up the waters, and whoever was first into the pool after such a disturbance would be cured of whatever disease he had. In thirty-eight years the man had never managed to be the lucky one.

Jesus' question would seem to be a foolish one: the man was an invalid – why ask him whether he wanted to be cured? Of course he did; anyone would want to be cured. I wonder how deeply Jesus saw into that man's soul. After all that time, he knew no other life than that of an invalid. Indeed, in Israel in those days, with no Welfare State to provide for him, the man was probably a beggar, and doubtless knew of no other way of making a living. A beggar with an obvious disability would be a more likely candidate for receiving charity from kindly passers-by; if the man was healed, he might well lose some of his income!

I think that often, when we are in the depths of despair at our circumstances, and asking Jesus for help, he responds by asking us the same question: 'Do you want to be well?' Do we really want our circumstances to change, or have we become so accustomed to them that change would feel risky and unsafe? Are we willing to throw the crutch away and go unnoticed in the crowd? Or have we begun to enjoy the attention it gets us, the allowances that are made for us?

It is these ideas which have made me so wary of self-pity. I am determined not to make excuses for myself, and not to let other people make them for me. That way I avoid the temptation to become lazy, or self-centred or self-indulgent. That was why, for a while after Roy's funeral, I refused to wear black, in case it appeared that I was making a production out of mourning!

Even the worst of grief, however, is not entirely black. The first glimpse of this came on the Sunday evening after Roy died. I was at a Communion service at church, praising

God because we are told to 'praise him in everything' and that 'God inhabits the praises of his people'. I was thinking about Roy at the same time. Suddenly I saw a picture in my mind, of Roy and Jesus in a boat together, grinning and waving across the waves at me! I was praising Jesus and smiling at the same time, because it made me so happy to realise that Roy was united with his Lord. I thought, 'That's it! If I praise God with all my heart I will see Roy with Jesus and that will bring me comfort.' The next Sunday I was in church again, and I thought how wonderful it would be to experience that same feeling of reassurance and joy, knowing that Roy was safe and happy with Jesus. So I tried to recapture that picture, by praising Jesus in the same way as before. But this time the picture I saw was different: I seemed to see Roy and Jesus together, but turning their backs on me and walking away to something new. I realised that God never lets us stand still, and that already I had to be prepared to let Roy go, in my mind, into his new life. Nevertheless these pictures were a great source of comfort to me.

Another comfort was a verse from the Bible which leapt out at me with new meaning: 'Therefore, since we are surrounded with such a great cloud of witnesses, let us throw off everything that hinders and the sin that so easily entangles, and let us run with perseverance the race marked out for us' (Hebrews 12:1). I felt very strongly that this was a word meant for me at this time, all the more because my niece and several others also came across the same words and felt that they should pass them on to me.

Ever since then I have sensed Roy watching this life on earth, from the grandstand, as it were, with all the saints

– the great cloud of witnesses – cheering us on. At the same time I can look up to Roy and all the other Christians who have passed this way before me, and know that I am not alone in facing difficulties. They have run the race of faith before us and have made it by faith. Sometimes it fills me with longing to be able to talk to Roy, because he now sees Jesus face to face, and he knows the answers to many of my questions. Am I walking in the perfect will of God? What would he want me to do in certain situations? Sometimes I wish I could just phone him and ask him!

There is yet another side to self-awareness about grief: not only did I have to give myself permission to grieve, to weep when my tears were genuine grief and not self-pity, but I also had to give myself permission to be happy. Of course I am sad that Roy has died, and I miss him all the time. Yet we have always been a family that laughs a lot, and that hasn't changed. The children and I share many jokes; my heart lifts up when I praise Jesus and share in worship with other Christians; and on a day-to-day basis I am very contented. None of this means that I love and miss Roy any less.

There is a great temptation to feel guilty about being happy. It is almost as if grieving is a way of staying close to the loved one, and that to stop grieving – even for a minute – is disloyal, a suggestion that the loss doesn't matter. It isn't true, of course: quite the opposite. I know that Roy wants me to be happy, because he always wanted my life to be as good as possible, he always wanted the best for me. It was part of his love for me, and my love for him isn't changed in any way as I get on with the rest of my life.

Once again I had to exercise my will – my ability to choose how I would go through my grief. I would not wallow in self-pity, but I would allow myself to grieve honestly. I would not cling to sadness and depression, but I would allow myself to rejoice and give thanks for happiness and contentment, because they also are a gift from God.

8

Praying in God's Will

I suppose my greatest disappointment ever was that Roy was not completely healed from his cancer. At the end of his first course of treatment he seemed so well that I felt sure the final check-up would confirm his health. How we would rejoice when we told the world that he was healed! But when the results came back, they were inconclusive. Roy was very well, the tumour had disappeared off the x-ray completely, but a bronchoscopy revealed that there were still cancer cells in the lung. They might be dead, they might lie dormant, or they might start multiplying again. No one could say for sure how long Roy would remain well.

It was a bitter moment for me: I had been so sure that our prayers would be answered. Hadn't the Lord told me, right at the beginning of his illness, 'Stand back and see what I will do'? I had been so sure that God's plan for Roy would include his healing. After all we had been through, after all Roy had suffered through the early treatment, surely we *deserved* healing? That was when I realised how flawed and human my thinking was. Deep down, I was still thinking that we could deserve something – yet I knew that when we become Christians, we give up all rights to our own lives.

I had to repent of that kind of thinking. Long ago we had put our lives into God's hands, and had agreed to trust him for everything. Paul urges us 'to offer your bodies as living sacrifices, holy and pleasing to God – this is your spiritual act of worship' (Romans 12:1). We often pray, 'Lord, make my life a living sacrifice.' Then, when the Lord takes us at our word, we start whining. The fact is that we all hope that God's will for us entails no difficulties or dangers, no struggles for the body or the will. Yet how else is God to teach us the lessons of faithfulness and trust and love which he wants his children to learn?

It was through that great disappointment that I realised how much I still had to learn – lessons I knew in my head but not in my heart. When we give our lives to God we have to let go of our own desires and wills. I have worked this through for myself, often without realising it, in all the ups and downs of family life. All the time I was pressing for what I wanted, I was constantly frustrated by my inability to make the world revolve around my wants. But whenever I managed to put God first in my life, to say, 'All right, Lord, whatever you want' – then things began to work. Then I was able to experience the peace that comes from placing all our desires at the foot of the cross.

Right from the start Roy had been able to say, 'Well, this isn't the way I would have chosen, Lord, but it's your will, not mine – and if this is your will then it's OK by me.' That willingness to trust God takes the edge off all disappointments, fears and anxieties. Once I learned it life became easier. Then if God closed a door, I was able to accept it and wait for the next opportunity with patience, willing to see what God wanted me to do next.

When the family realised that Roy's cancer might come back, we committed ourselves afresh to Jesus, and to trusting him in everything. Certainly the time we had with Roy before he died was very precious, because we knew that it might be short: we made the most of every day. As Roy said once, 'I don't complain any more about standing on a station platform in the rain, because I'm glad to be alive to get wet!' Many years ago we read a very funny book by Bill Cosby, in which he described his elderly parents going for a walk together, stopping for a rest on a bench, and his father taking off his hat and accidentally sitting on it. It became a private joke; Roy would say 'When I sit on my hat . . .' meaning when he was very elderly and absent-minded. He always wanted us to enjoy old age together.

One of the things I am very grateful for is that I had the privilege of two and a half years with Roy after his cancer was first diagnosed. In that time I was able to say to him everything I needed to say, and to tell him how grateful I was to him for being such a good and faithful husband and father. I do not suffer from regret in the sense of feeling that we had any unfinished business between us. It must be very hard for those whose loved ones die suddenly and without warning, because so much is left unsaid.

Far worse must be those situations where the relationship has been difficult. If Roy's cancer had been diagnosed before I became a Christian, I am sure the trauma would have been much greater, because I would have felt so guilty. In those early years when I suffered from depression I wasn't easy to live with, and I found it hard to share my feelings: Roy must often have felt shut out. Once I had committed my life to Jesus and experienced the love and peace of God, we got better at talking about everything, and our marriage improved as a result.

Our relationship wasn't perfect, of course, and we had our ups and downs and all the day-to-day irritations of any family. Roy's father used to laugh when he heard people say, 'We've been married fifty years and we've never had a cross word.' He would say, in his inimitable Yorkshire accent, 'If there's never an argument, somebody's the underdog!' Roy and I learned from our disagreements, though: we learned 'not to let the sun go down on our anger', and how to talk things through, so that we never left resentments to fester or little problems to grow. Most of all, we shared our faith in Jesus, so that our marriage had a common aim: to live in God's will. We were very happy together. That was why, when we knew that Roy was dying, there was no need to express anything except sadness. There were no old wounds to heal, nothing to apologise for, no harsh words to wish unsaid.

It is yet another example of the importance of living in God's will every day, because we never know what is around the corner. None of us knows what lies ahead, so we have to take to heart the advice of the old farmer: to 'farm as if you are going to live for ever, and live as though you are going to die tomorrow'.

At Spring Harvest Steve Chalke told a story about Roy

which illustrated this. At Pentecost 1994 there was a nationwide Christian campaign called 'On Fire', and Roy was asked to appear at Central Hall, Westminster, as part of the 'On Fire for London' events. He insisted on going, although he was very ill at the time, and in fact during the main part of the meeting he fainted backstage. Afterwards, however, he was well enough to attend the Press Conference, and one of the reporters asked him how it felt, knowing that he had only three months to live.

'Knowing that I have three months to live would make me the most privileged person in this room,' he replied. 'Why's that? responded the reporter. ''Cos you don't know if you've got tomorrow!' Roy knew that no one can really plan for the future: he knew the verses in the Bible that tell us so:

> Now listen, you who say, 'Today or tomorrow we will go to this or that city, spend a year there, carry on business and make money.' Why, you do not even know what will happen tomorrow. What is your life? You are a mist that appears for a little while and then vanishes. Instead, you ought to say, 'If it is the Lord's will, we will live and do this or that.' As it is, you boast and brag. (James 4:13–16)

I believe that it was the power of the Holy Spirit which enabled Roy to face all his suffering without bitterness or regrets. When his lung cancer was diagnosed, he realised that it was the kind of cancer which is usually found in heavy smokers – yet he himself had never smoked a cigarette in his life. However, he had worked for many years in smoky nightclubs, inhaling deeply when he played the trumpet, sang or danced. 'Passive smoking' – inhaling the smoke from other people's cigarettes – was the only explanation his doctors could offer. As a result of this, he not only campaigned tirelessly to raise funds for research into lung cancer, but also spoke out about the dangers of smoking and passive smoking.

This gift of the Holy Spirit which preserves us from indulging in bitterness and regrets is very precious. It is part of the promise, 'the Lord your God goes with you; he will never leave you nor forsake you' (Deuteronomy 31:6) and it is this which keeps us safe in the midst of danger. 'Safe' may not mean physical safety, but the security which holds our spirits and keeps us from despair.

Sometimes I liken our relationship with Jesus to an insurance policy, which doesn't prevent burglaries or burst water pipes, but enables us to deal with the consequences! When Roy did his record-breaking wing-walking stunt, standing strapped to the roof of a light aircraft as it flew across the English Channel, the BBC insured him for a million pounds. This was not a good-luck charm to keep him safe, but a precaution to deal with the results of a possible disaster – to pay for the support of an invalid or widow if accident or death resulted. Christians do not lead charmed lives. We are as susceptible as anyone else to accident, difficulty or tragedy. Jesus says that when we follow him he will not keep us safe *from* trouble, but safe *in* trouble: he does not protect his children from misfortune, but whatever the difficulties, he will be with us and uphold us.

This becomes all the more real when we are facing up to death or the fear of death: how can we endure it? That is when we cash in the insurance policy, and all the riches of Jesus' love are placed in our hands, and the power of the Holy Spirit, the Comforter, is at our disposal. 'The peace of God, which transcends all understanding, will guard your hearts and your minds in Christ Jesus' (Philippians 4:7). This seems to me to sum it up: if our hearts and minds remain stable, fixed firmly and secure, then we will not be disturbed by events, however dreadful. And we can only be 'kept' in the knowledge and love of God by his word, as we study to understand it and to work it out daily in our lives.

So if we call upon the power of the Holy Spirit to release us from bitterness, what of the disappointments? How can we understand how these things fit together? What about all our unanswered prayers and unfulfilled hopes? My greatest prayer and longing was for Roy to be restored to his family in full health, so why wasn't Roy healed?

The most painful answer to this question, and one which has been suggested to me on more than one occasion, is that we didn't have enough faith. Many Christians seem to subscribe to the view that it is always God's will that everyone should be healed, and that miraculous healing is prevented only by our failure to believe. I find this a difficult area, for I have personally known both people who have experienced healing, and others who have not. While it is certainly true that sometimes people are healed miraculously, I do not think that we can assume that we can predict God's purposes in all cases, just because an outcome seems desirable to our human minds.

Moreover, it is tragic that people who are already suffering should be hurt by other Christians who criticise them for not having enough faith. Certainly both Roy and I had to make a conscious effort to let go of the feelings of hurt and guilt that this sort of suggestion aroused in us. Such feelings are counter-productive – they waste time and precious emotional energy, because even if the accusation were true, there would be little we could do about it! Roy's response was to say, 'Let's not worry about it. God knows my heart, better than I do. Sorry, God, if I'm wrong, and if I don't have enough faith. All I can do is trust you.' We were reminded of the man in the Bible who asked Jesus to heal his son. Jesus said to him, 'Everything is possible for him who believes.' Immediately the man replied, 'I do believe; help me overcome my unbelief!' (Mark 9:24)

In any case, I think this criticism that we have insufficient faith is too glib, too simplistic. It treats God as though he were a slot-machine from which you can get anything you order, if you only insert enough faith coins. We know that our God is not mechanical, but a loving Father, and we can know him personally and trust him, even when things are going badly for us. God is sovereign in our circumstances and we can trust him to bring about his will.

It comforted us to know that other, greater Christians than us had received similar criticism. David Watson, who died of cancer, went through similar problems; Selwyn Hughes wrote movingly in *Every Day with Jesus* about the death of his wife, and those Bible study notes helped me to come to terms with my own situation.

From time to time another similar suggestion is made: that healing cannot take place when there is insufficient prayer. A man whose daughter had cancer wrote to many churches, asking people to pray for her, as though he could achieve his desire simply by collecting enough prayers. Even though I sympathise with his feelings, I cannot go along with this idea, either. Prayer isn't a commodity that you can pile up. In any case, God is never going to say, 'You didn't have enough.' He will heal, if it is his will, in response to one person's prayer.

No one could have had more prayer than Roy. His position as a well-known celebrity meant that thousands of Christians heard of his illness and prayed for him. Even among our own local community, so many people told our pastor, Jim Graham, that they were praying for Roy, that Jim said he could imagine God saying, 'Oh, do you know him as well?' I know we were supported and encouraged by all those prayers, but I am also sure that God isn't influenced by such inequality as how famous someone is! God shares the pain and cares for all his suffering children, no matter how many or how few their friends.

> Are not two sparrows sold for a penny? Yet not one of them will fall to the ground apart from the will of your Father. And even the very hairs of your head are all numbered. So don't be afraid; you are worth more than many sparrows (Matthew 10:29).

I do believe that for all of us there is a time to die, and that God's purposes and timing may not be fully understood by us as we operate on our human scale. Many people have said to me how sad it was that Roy should die so young, and that he should die before his time. My response is that he did not die before his time – that those were his allotted days. In the graveyard of Grewelthorpe village church, Yorkshire, there is a memorial to a girl who died at the age of seventeen. It says, 'She asked life of thee, and thou gavest her a long life, even for ever and ever.'

In the case of long-drawn-out illness, we often experience great relief when the pain is over, and God takes the sufferer to be with him. A friend whose little daughter died wrote to say that it would be selfish of us to want our loved ones back, 'because they are experiencing something so wonderful with Jesus.' The problem is always that we view our situation with our human eyes, and the limitations of our human time-scheme. We are grieving for our own loss of expectations. God has greater purposes to fulfil, which often we cannot comprehend.

It is only now, with hindsight, that I can begin to make sense of the fact that Roy was not healed of his cancer. Of course, healing would have been a tremendous witness to the miracle-working power of God (and the wisdom and skills of the doctors who fought the battle against cancer with Roy are also a part of that power). Yet God had other purposes in mind. If Roy had been healed, that would have been wonderful; yet many others daily are not healed – would they have been helped by our victory? Perhaps, but I cannot help thinking that they were helped far more by the fact that Roy trusted God for the outcome and continued to have faith and hope right to the end. A complete cure would have set him apart. Because his case was 'ordinary' like theirs, other sufferers can identify with him. His story can encourage them to understand that with the help of the Holy Spirit, a person can face even death with confidence and joy. That was the door that God was opening for us: the opportunity to touch lives with the witness to God's power to support us in our daily lives however dire the circumstances.

Because of this, I am nowadays very careful about how I pray about things. In the final stages of Roy's illness some dear friends were still praying for his healing. I was perplexed about the right thing to do, so I said, 'Lord, I will pray one more time for this, and after that I will not ask any more.' When I did so, I felt that I had a clear message in my heart from God: 'No, I will not heal Roy; but I am with you and that is all you need.' Immediately I felt at peace about it, and knew that I need not be concerned any more. I did not want to be praying for something that God did not want for us – I did not want to be outside his will. Shortly before this a group of us had gathered one evening to pray for Roy, who was then suffering great pain. As we prayed I had an amazing sense of God's timelessness, and felt that he was speaking to me and saying, 'What are days? What are years? Roy will not die before the time I have appointed for him. His life is in my hands. I will have fulfilled my purposes through Roy. Release him to me, set him free because the battle has been won through the prayers of the faithful. There is no guilt and there is no failure, because I am the Lord of time. Rest in the knowledge that the day I choose will be the right day. Don't be afraid – don't you realise that your loss is my gain?' The sense of peace and joy in my heart that evening was immeasurable; we needed to feel no remorse or guilt, only joy and trust that God's will would be done on earth, as it is in heaven.

Some of our prayers and longings have to be given up when we give our lives to Jesus; we have to let go of our own desires and wills. This is never easy, because it does not come naturally to any of us: we find it hard truly to submit our will to God. At our church we often sing a hymn which includes the line, 'Here I am, wholly available'. I want to be able to sing it, but usually I end up singing, 'Here I am, *fairly* available' – well, there is no point in being less than honest, and God knows me only too well!

I am working at it, though: deep down I really do want to do what God wants. To be ready for whatever he wants me to do, I feel that I need to live simply, and get rid of all the trappings and encumbrances: I am not a hoarder, and I don't want to keep things for sentimental reasons – they only gather dust! Selwyn Hughes says that there are two ways of being rich: we can be rich 'in the abundance of our possessions' or 'in the fewness of our wants'. For the Christian, I think the second kind of wealth is better. I greatly admired the pope who said, towards the end of his life, 'My bags are packed and I am ready to go.' I should like to feel like that now. Catherine Marshall, a great Christian writer, told about sorting papers after the death of her father.

Then I picked up Dad's final bank statement. I could scarcely believe what I was seeing. His balance was sixty-five cents.

It is true that you can't take it with you. But whoever heard of someone coming out *that* even at the end of life?

How typical of Dad! He never did have any money. The salaries of preachers in small towns are notoriously small. Yet always he had been supplied with every need – even to a college education for each of his children and Evergreen Farm for his retirement. His sixty-five-cent statement somehow seemed right.[1]

This seems to me to be the right attitude. Jesus warns us of placing too much faith in worldly possessions in the story of the man who reaped a specially good harvest: he planned to pull down his barns and build bigger ones, and prepare for a wealthy retirement.

> But God said to him, 'You fool! This very night your life will be demanded from you. Then who will get what you have prepared for yourself?' This is how it will be with anyone who stores up things for himself but is not rich towards God (Luke 12:20–21).

I am keen now to get all my affairs in order so that when I die, my children won't have too much to do. When Roy was alive we talked about this, and decided that should we live to a ripe old age, we didn't want to be a nuisance to the children. So while we were still of 'sound mind', we composed a letter to each of them, telling them so. We said that they all had their own lives to live, and they were not to spend time looking after us or visiting us: if necessary they should put us into a nursing home, and not feel guilty about it, because they had in writing what we wanted. Di Parsons joked with us that her children had caused her so much hassle as teenagers, that she intended to live as long as possible to get her own back!

My other great longing is to die in harness; to go on being useful to the Lord right to the end, and not to fade

---

[1] Catherine Marshall, *Beyond Our Selves*, Hodder & Stoughton 1969

away or become a burden to the children. I am grateful that Roy, in spite of the suffering he went through during his illness, nevertheless did not suffer the lingering indignities of old age, or the physical infirmities he would have found it so hard to bear. Rob and Di Parsons often visited us during Roy's illness, and knew him well. Rob says he felt that God compressed the final years of Roy's life into two years, giving them a sharp focus and an impact on people which would never have happened if he had died peacefully of old age.

We may never know the truth about God's mysterious ways until this life is over and we see him face to face. Until then, much of what we think and do is a kind of guessing about his purposes. But I believe that only the love of God and the comfort of the Holy Spirit can help us to see that what may appear as a disappointment to us can in fact be a part of God's perfect plan for our lives.

9
Living With Grief

The first instinct of grief is very often hibernation. You want to curl up and hide away from others while you struggle to get used to this new state. However, in the first weeks after Roy died I found myself caught up in a whirl of activity. It wasn't just the usual tasks of informing friends and arranging the funeral: there was mail by the sackful and the constant attention of the press. The letters and cards were full of love and consolation, and the requests for interviews were from many journalists who had supported Roy throughout his illness. However, the volume of demands was overwhelming: it was all very tiring.

Grieving is an exhausting process, and I remember that a lot of the time I felt absolutely spent and drained. I was not really surprised by this. I have always been a very active person – my ballet training ensured that I was always very fit and energetic – but I remember that when my mother died, even though it was not unexpected, I seemed to have no energy. I used to get to the top of the stairs with my legs tingling and my muscles weak and floppy, and I would have to lie down on the landing before I could go on, hoping that no one would follow me before I was upright again! Bereavement is always stressful, no matter how well prepared we think we are, or how well we think we are coping. And stress is like an illness: we need to rest and allow the body time to recover.

At the time of Roy's death, Ben had been ill with a tummy bug, and I picked up the same virus almost at once. I felt sick with kidney pains, but I knew that if I told anyone, they would assume that I was suffering from stress. I was, of course, but I knew that wasn't what was causing my illness, because it so closely mirrored Ben's. So I told no one; I didn't want anyone telling me that I was cracking up already! By the time of the funeral I hadn't eaten anything much for three days. However, I did find that I could eat small pieces of a chocolate cake brought as a gift by a friend, so I indulged in that. I did allow myself a little comfort-eating from time to time: when you are grieving you have to be kind to yourself, and not expect too much too soon.

Shortly after Roy's death was announced on the television news, there was a ring at the front door. It was a neighbour: the man who runs the Indian restaurant up the road from us, where Roy and I had often eaten in the past. Roy thought it an excellent restaurant, and often took business people there for lunch, because he loved the curry. The proprietor said how sorry he was to hear of Roy's death.

'It is the custom in our culture,' he said, 'at a time of death, for the neighbours to bring in food for the family.

We consider you our neighbour and we would like to cook for you.'

I was very touched by this gesture, and began to say to him, 'It's very kind of you, but please don't bother.' But I was drowned out by the children behind me in the hall, chorusing, 'Oh, yes, please, that would be wonderful!' So for the next two days we had Indian takeaways delivered, which were much appreciated. This kind man is a Muslim, but to show his respect for Roy he attended the funeral in our church. Our hearts were warmed by the dignity and caring of these gifts to us – his presence as well as the food.

Grieving is hard work, for the body as well as for the emotions, and we need to allow for that. It's so easy to drive ourselves from one task to the next, in an effort to keep busy and perhaps not to think too much about things. I found just the opposite: I needed to be able to think, to take stock of the situation and come to terms with the fact of Roy's death. I needed rest, and I had to take care not to let events carry me on so fast that I didn't have time for that. Similarly, it's easy to feel so churned up by our feelings that we don't eat properly; in fact, our bodies need proper food as much as rest to get on with life. These gestures of practical love from our Muslim neighbour helped me to remember this.

Even so, there were times when everyday tasks threatened to overwhelm me. There were things people used to ask Roy to do – write letters, collect cheques, say a few words to thank fund-raisers – and now they began to ask me to do them. They needed someone to take over Roy's position in the limelight. One day I suddenly realised,

'I'm trying to be Roy *and* me – I'm doing two people's work here!' and after that it became easier to understand, at least, why I was so tired.

For instance, Roy's book, *Now and Then*, was due to be published two weeks after his death. I realised that this made things rather difficult for his publishers, Robson Books, so I said casually, 'If there's anything I can do, just ask' – not thinking for a minute that there would be anything I could do to help them. But in fact it seemed that many people wanted me to give interviews to publicise the book: something that would have been no effort for Roy, but was a new and taxing experience for me.

I often thought, 'If only Roy were here to give me a few tips on what to say, how not to seem nervous in front of the microphone, how to make little jokes to relax people,' but of course if he were, I wouldn't have needed his help! Sometimes it made me feel very lonely.

At one stage, when I was missing Roy dreadfully, I was reading in my Bible study notes about the joy which awaits Christians when we finally see the Lord. 'That's all very well, Jesus,' I said, 'but at this moment I'd rather see Roy!' (Jesus knows our hearts better than we do ourselves, so we have to be real when we're talking to him.) The next day the study notes directed me to Isaiah 54:4–5; 'Remember no more the reproach of your widowhood. For your Maker is your husband – the Lord Almighty is his name – the Holy One of Israel is your Redeemer.' What an answer to my heart's cry: he knew and understood my pain. I remember that when things get on top of me, and I feel lonely and sad. I also have conversations with him: 'OK, Jesus, if Roy were here he'd help me with this . . . if you're my husband you have to help me make decisions!'

There was one day shortly after this when I received out of the blue a most unpleasant and abusive letter which upset me so much that I burst into tears. There was no one to share it with, no one to tell me not to bother about it, and for a while I felt really low. Later that day I had to go to a school prizegiving, and I really needed to be pleasant and cheerful, not moping and sad, so I tried sharing it with the Lord. How should I deal with it? Immediately my thoughts ran on: was I going to let one horrid letter colour my whole weekend? How important was it, anyway, in the light of eternity? Fortunately God gives us a sense of proportion, and I realised that I would be foolish to allow depression even a foothold that day: I decided not to think about it any more. It may seem a small victory over loneliness, but it proved to me that the words in Isaiah could be true for me, and that Jesus could meet my needs, even when I missed my husband's companionship the most.

Once again I realised how important it is not to give way to self-pity. I try on the whole not to rely too much on other people; they have troubles of their own, and though I have many good friends to whom I can go for help with difficulties, I try to keep my troubles to myself. I want to be positive and cheerful when I am with others (and keep my friends!): there's nothing more unattractive than people who are always 'awfulising' everything. I think that I have slowly learned how to get on and cope with life alone – after all, single people who have never married do it all the time. It isn't particularly heroic, only difficult for those of us who have become accustomed to having someone to share our lives.

When Roy died I felt as though I had been cut in two – and in a sense I had. When two people marry, they become 'one flesh', sharing everything. When one partner dies, half of that one flesh is torn away, and the other does indeed feel like only half a person. I have now become a whole person again: the Lord's healing oil makes the wound heal up more quickly.

Perhaps this is harder for those women whose husbands have regular jobs – or no jobs – whose lives together have involved regular, consistent contact. At least I wasn't used to that; throughout our marriage we had no routine at all: sometimes Roy was working from home, at others he would be away for weeks on end. Before I became a Christian I found this very difficult, but afterwards I became more confident and able to cope. Now I am thankful that I had to develop that small degree of independence, because I am to some extent used to being on my own. I am so grateful to God for preparing me in advance.

In fact, it was almost tempting to slip into the old routines I established when Roy was away working: I had to make myself aware that Roy was never coming back, and force myself to face the pain of that fact. Curiously, this burden of loneliness feels heaviest not at funerals (when I might perhaps expect to feel sad) but at weddings. When a friend's son married soon after Roy died I was greatly moved by the teaching in the service: the minister spoke about relationships, and how they build up over the years, so that an established marriage founded on Christ is a strong building indeed. Our experience was just that, and my sense of loss was intense; I cried all the way through the service – but not at all at a memorial service which I attended later the same day.

Another emotion which can be overwhelming in bereavement is anger: many people have asked me whether I feel angry with God for 'letting' Roy get cancer. I have to admit that anger has not been one of my emotions. If we trust God, and believe that he has a plan for our lives, then there isn't any point in getting angry with him if things don't work out quite the way we would have liked. We have to submit to his will, and trust that he is working out his purposes for a greater good that we are not yet able to see with our earthbound eyes.

Although I tend not to get angry with God, I am perfectly capable of feeling very irritated with people – especially those who make what I consider to be offering glib, superficially comforting remarks. There were people who said to me, 'Remember, Roy is not far away from you – he's only next door' I wanted to retort, 'If he were only next door don't you think I'd be there with him?' I refrained, though. I also make a huge effort not to take things too personally, especially when people make insensitive comments. I was chatting to a man once whose wife had gone away for ten days to visit relatives; he complained that he was having trouble sleeping, that he hated being in the bed alone, and generally was immensely miserable. I could easily have become sentimental and angry; didn't I have a right to be much more miserable than he was? His problem was only going to last for ten days, mine was for ever. I chose not to react and changed the subject!

However, I know many people who suffer from powerful feelings of anger when someone they love suffers or dies, and I'm sure that it is a perfectly normal reaction. It is essential to express it and get it out of our system; it's important to face up to all these strong emotions, deal with them and get rid of them, because if we repress them they only make their way out in physical symptoms of stress, which do our bodies no good.

In the end, the only people hurt by our anger are ourselves (though if we go around snapping at everyone all day there may be some hurt feelings around to deal with!). The best thing to do, as with all such destructive emotions which seem to be beyond our control, is to dump them at the foot of the cross. God can cope with our anger, our hatred, our bitterness and resentment and any other unattractive feelings we are ashamed of: we can't tell him anything he doesn't know already. And he is always waiting for us to admit our weakness, confess the times we have given in to our resentment and fury and taken it out on other people, and tell him we are sorry and ready to start again. Indeed, we cannot start again until we do come to that point of admitting where we have failed. Jim Graham likens this to a foul in a football match: once the foul has been committed and we have recognised it, the referee's whistle has blown. After that it doesn't matter how long we go on playing – there can be no score until the players return to the place where the foul was committed and start again. Similarly, we cannot move forward in our life with God until we go back and confess the sin and accept God's forgiveness.

I recall hearing a radio interview in which someone said, 'Pure joy comes only through the heartbreak of Calvary' and I believe that this is true. It is the joy of release which enables us to be free and not burdened by our sins, the joy of faith which knows that God is in charge of our world. It bubbles up in spite of all our circumstances because it is an eternal joy which is not transitory nor due to any particular circumstances of our lives.

Once, after I had given a talk about my experiences of marriage and bereavement, a lady came up and told me that since her husband died she had suffered from feelings of anger, bitterness and resentment. I told her that it was all right to experience common human emotions, for we are all human; and that whenever I felt them I placed them at the foot of the cross and gave them over to Jesus. I suggested that when she prayed she should ask Jesus to replace those emotions with the power of the Holy Spirit, and with his love, joy and peace. That night I prayed for her, but I didn't expect to hear from her again. The next day I travelled to Ayr in Scotland, and was surprised to find a fax waiting for me at the office I was going to. It was from my friend from the day before, and said, 'Dear Fiona, it worked! I sat at the feet of Jesus and he bathed me with his peace.'

'The nights of doubt and worry' are another burden of bereavement. When Roy was alive he was the main decision-maker in our family, and I found the new pressure on me to make decisions alone was stressful. For the first few days I even found making decisions about the funeral difficult, though the family and church were wonderful. They sorted out the flowers in the church, the physical arrangements for the service, and even liaised with Sky TV who were televising the service live, so that I didn't have to worry about anything. The afternoon before the service I went down to the church with a bunch of helium balloons and found the place a hive of activity: the whole congregation had swung into action and everyone was working as a team, relieving me of any anxiety about the organisation.

In the old days Roy had always teased me about being 'a cushion plumper' – meaning someone who goes round last thing at night plumping up the cushions and making sure everything is nice for the next day. When I became a Christian I learned not to worry about being ready for tomorrow. As Roy used to say, 'Get on with your life, but don't forget to smell the roses on the way.' It is a waste of time and energy to worry about the future, because we can't see it or plan for it, and it's pointless to worry about what might never happen. Before I became a Christian I used to worry about everything; now I just pray about everything and trust in God to help me. I try to practise a verse from Philippians:

> 'Don't worry about anything; instead, pray about everything; tell God your needs and don't forget to thank him for his answers. If you do this you will experience God's peace, which is far more wonderful than the human mind can understand' (Philippians 4:6–7, *Living Bible*).

Curiously, when we had real trouble in our lives, I believe that God prepared me for it, so that when Roy's second bout of cancer began, I was not surprised – just disappointed. We had already learned to trust God one day at a time, and not to look further. Some of those nights were very dark indeed. There were moments when I asked, 'Where is God in all this?' – times when he didn't seem to be answering our prayers or taking away Roy's suffering. That was when I felt most alone, as though I was in a dark tunnel and there was no way out but to keep plodding forward without hope or help or light. Three months afterwards I spent a quiet day's retreat at Highmoor Hall, and came across this piece by Ulrich Shaeffer, which perfectly reflected my feelings at this time.

My outstretched hands are becoming accustomed
to the solitude into which you have thrown me
more alone
than I could ever bear to be

I am learning to live
with the death you have chosen for me
more painful than any death
I have ever chosen to go through

My eyes are adapting
to the darkness you have chosen for me
darker than any darkness
I ever knew or chose

I am learning to recognise
the many disguises of your love
deeper than any love
I have ever experienced

And slowly it dawns on me
Being lonely is: turning to you
death is: a deep and joyous life
darkness is: finally seeing your light
and love is: being born over and over again.[1]

Again, back in the days before I was a Christian I was always a prey to worries and fears, and when Roy was away (which was often) I was frequently unable to sleep. After I became a Christian I learned the secret of not worrying, but trusting in God and resting in him. 'I will lie down in peace and sleep, for though I am alone, O Lord, you will keep me safe' (Psalm 4:8, *Living Bible*). I would pray each night, 'Lord, please will you wrap me in your loving arms,' and then I would find it easy to fall asleep.

Generally, my feeling about sleeplessness is that the best thing is to get up and do something, and not let it worry you: if you aren't asleep you probably don't need to be, and lying awake worrying about it doesn't help. Insomnia is nearly always linked to stress and being unable to relax; a hot drink, a good book and being resigned to being awake often does the trick!

My favourite story about insomnia was told by Clive Calver at yet another Spring Harvest. It was during the Blitz in London: night after night people would go down into the air raid shelters, and what with the fear and worry and the distant noises of bombs and sirens, few would be able to get much sleep. One little old lady, however, was always able to settle down and sleep peacefully. When

---

[1] Ulrich Schaffer, *Into Your Light*, InterVarsity Press

someone asked her how she did it, she replied, 'I used to find it hard to sleep down here. So I prayed about it, and God said to me, "I'm awake all night anyway; there's no point in both of us being up!" '

No matter what the burdens we have to carry each day, or what worries beset us at night, we have the comfort of knowing that Jesus is there beside us to take all our cares upon himself and release us into confidence, joy and peace. For all these things, we have Jesus – what a wonderful friend.

10
Facing the Future

Bereavement is a strange experience: as I look back over the years since Roy died, some events seem incredibly immediate, while others have almost faded from my memory. For the first two years or so, it felt as if everything had happened only yesterday. Every moment was vivid in my memory and I felt raw and bruised – like half a person. Nowadays it all seems such a long time ago. And I feel complete as a single woman once again.

On the first anniversary of Roy's death I received many cards remembering him, and I was very moved that so many people took the time to think of me. Jim Graham, our pastor, and his wife Anne sent me some flowers with the simple message, 'With deep gratitude for precious memories of the past and certain glorious hope for the future', and that made me cry, because they remembered him with love and the memories were precious to them. 'Hope for the future' was exactly right, too, because part of the challenge of bereavement is the need to face the future alone with hope.

There were dark times when I was weary and sad and I missed Roy dreadfully, but I also tried to be cheerful and busy. I took the time to think about him, and I did not try to escape in any way from the reality of bereavement. However, I didn't want to spend the rest of my life dwelling on thoughts of death and widowhood. Sometimes I did feel a pang of guilt that I didn't seem to be 'mourning' in the traditional sense, but with a lively young family and a busy church life, I would have made everyone's lives miserable if I insisted on sitting at home and doing nothing but grieving.

There may be many bad times when we need reassurance: then, the Bible tells us, 'Be joyful always; pray continually; give thanks in all circumstances, for this is God's will for you in Christ Jesus' (1 Thessalonians 5: 16–18). It may be hard for us to give thanks *for* the bad times, but we can at least give thanks *in* the bad times, and often when we make that effort we find that our attitude is transformed. Simply putting God back into the heart of our circumstances is often enough to restore our sense of proportion and enable us to see a way through. I know that if I praise God when things are bad, I am often lifted out of my dark mood and given the grace to see things with God's eternal perspective – it's amazing how small some of our concerns can seem then. It also reassures me by restoring my faith in his overall plan for my life; I find it exciting that his plan for me is still unfolding, and I marvel at what he does, and at the unique opportunities which emerge when we let God have his way.

Before I became a Christian I knew a lot about what the Bible says, but had no more thought of putting it into action than of speaking in Hebrew. It never occurred to me that the Bible could be relevant to my everyday life; I thought it was an informative story about what happened a long time ago, a long way away. Now I realise that the Bible is God's word for us, and it tells us how to live and how to follow Jesus in our daily life, but it isn't any help to us unless we are prepared to act on its instructions.

I liken it to studying a Rosemary Conley fitness plan: we can read about keeping fit, look at the sets of exercises to improve our muscles, and check out the diet sheets and recipes. We can see what an excellent system the whole thing is – but we won't get any fitter unless we actually do the exercises, throw away the cream buns and keep to the plan. In the same way we can read God's word every day, but it's no good just agreeing with it; unless we are prepared to put it into practice we won't change our lives and we won't realise that it works.

Following Jesus is challenging: some of the jobs I have been asked to do in the last few years have astonished me – and often my first reaction has been to say, 'I can't possibly do that!' But I decided early on that I would take opportunities as they were offered. I didn't want to have regrets later, or wonder what would have happened if I'd only had the courage to try. Even more, at the end of my life I didn't want to hear God say, 'Where were you when I needed you?' I remember someone saying in a television interview, 'I'd rather fail while daring valiantly than never do anything at all.' I decided it was better to risk failure by trying to rise to the challenges God set me.

I have approached some of these challenges with great trepidation and shaking with nerves, but later I have been

144

glad I made the attempt. For example, I am sometimes asked to speak at medical conferences on behalf of carers. At first I thought this was ridiculous – I have no medical knowledge, and couldn't possibly tell all those doctors and nurses anything they didn't know already. However, I could speak of my experiences of caring for Roy throughout his illness, and I do know what it's like to be on the receiving end of the system! I have been amazed at how responsive and supportive the audiences have been. I have also been able to write a book, *Cancer's a Word, not a Sentence*, a positive and supportive guide for cancer patients, their families and friends.[1] One consultant who read it said to me that he would never again think of the patient in Bed 4 just as a carcinoma, but as a person with feelings and emotions.

Even before Roy died I had begun to speak at outreach events such as Christian Viewpoint, and a few conferences. Sometimes I am presenting the Christian message to people who have scarcely heard it, or supporting and encouraging Christians who are faithfully trying to walk in God's way. Sometimes people come and pour out their personal sorrows, and all I can do is listen to them, and give them my time and attention, and show the love of Jesus for them in that way. Through this work I meet people I would never otherwise have met or been involved with, and I thank God for the opportunities he gives me.

My favourite audience is one consisting of young

[1] Fiona Castle with Jan Greenough, *Cancer's a Word, not a Sentence*, Hodder & Stoughton 2000

mothers, because then I am usually speaking from my own experience of bringing up a family of four. I love to see the recognition in their faces when they realise that they are not the only ones with certain feelings, or who behave in a certain way. I cheerfully recount some of my worst mistakes, and enjoy their laughter, and seeing the little whispered conversations springing up as they share in my experiences. I feel very close to young mothers and want to encourage them; often their work goes unnoticed and unappreciated and their self-esteem is low. I think it is so important to build up their sense of self-worth, for in bringing up the next generation they are engaged in the most important work of all. They need to be affirmed in their role of homemaker and mother, something society doesn't do these days: they are made to feel like second-class citizens if they are not earning money outside the home.

My own family is still very important to me: I now have two lovely grandsons (Christopher and Jonathan) provided by Daniel and his Norwegian wife, Birthe. Daniel teaches at a Christian language school, and Birthe is a full-time mother. Julia, my older daughter, is still working in Peru with Latin Link, a missionary organisation operating in Latin America, and we keep in touch by frequent emails. Antonia and Benjamin both work in show business, Antonia as a locations manager with the BBC, and Benjamin as a professional musician playing saxophone, clarinet and flute. All four have come to know Jesus as their Saviour.

When I first became a Christian I came across a special verse in the Bible: 'I will instruct you (says the Lord) and guide you along the best pathway for your life; I will advise you and watch your progress' (Psalm 32:8, *Living Bible*). I took this as a personal sign for my life, but I was also challenged to take it on board for my children. Not only does God have a plan for my life, but he also knows the best pathway for them. Suddenly I felt released from the pressure of society's demands for dazzling exam results, top jobs and good incomes. My greatest ambition for them is simply that they should be walking in God's will, and it gives me great joy to be beside them as they discover God's blessings for them.

At home I keep a picture of Roy on the landing halfway up the stairs, and as I pass it on my way upstairs I often stop, kiss my fingers and touch them to Roy's face – it's a little gesture that's important to me. But sometimes I'm in such a hurry that I gallop upstairs two at a time and call out, 'Sorry, can't stop – too busy!' I know Roy would enjoy that – it's partly his fault I'm so busy in the first place! I also get quite tired with all the travelling and speaking, but I am amazed that when I am doing what God wants, I always seem to have enough energy to go round. I may go to bed absolutely exhausted, but I always wake with a spring in my heel and my energy renewed. 'Those who hope in the Lord will renew their strength. They will soar on wings like eagles; they will run and not grow weary, they will walk and not be faint' (Isaiah 40:31).

All this is part of being willing to look for what God wants us to do, and then going for it, however weak we may think we are. Our ability or lack of it is of little account when God is in charge – he enables us to do his will; the crucial part for us is getting on with it!

One interesting development has been the growth of bereavement conferences and seminars, both for professionals and for ordinary people. Care for the Family asked me to speak at a weekend conference for bereaved parents, and as usual my first response was that I couldn't possibly do it, because I had no experience of their situation. I was not a bereaved parent and could not understand their pain. However, I was persuaded to attend, and I took the opportunity to sit in on the seminars and listen to the speakers and the parents' responses. I realised then that although the circumstances of bereavement may be different, the emotions and reactions are very similar. The process and the feelings are often much the same, whatever the reasons. When I spoke to them I gave instances of my own feelings, but I guarded against saying 'I know how you feel' because I don't know how anyone else feels.

I remember being very irritated by people who said this to me when I was newly bereaved. First there were the predictors of gloom, who seemed to have fixed ideas about how people should react to situations. A widowed friend of mine was told by a counsellor, 'You must be very angry,' to which she responded, 'Why? How can you tell me how I should feel?' In my case lots of people told me that I wasn't sufficiently depressed after Roy's death. It seems rather hard to be criticised publicly for cheerfulness!

Then there were the instructors, who made dogmatic statements like, 'You should never move house soon after being bereaved.' I knew within days of Roy's death that I wanted to move, and never changed my mind, even though I took their advice and waited a while. I understand that uprooting yourself soon after a loved one has died might not be the best thing – specially since bereavement and moving house both score highly on a scale of stress-inducing activities! – but I knew that it was right for me, and so it has proved to be. My new neighbours are friendly and kind, and I no longer have the responsibility of running a larger house.

The point is that there is no blueprint for going through bereavement: we all have different coping mechanisms, different strengths and weaknesses, and different emotional baggage which we bring with us. Even though we experience similar emotions, everyone tackles them in different ways. I recently heard an interview with a lady-in-waiting to Queen Elizabeth the Queen Mother. When her husband died she asked the widowed Queen Mother: 'Does it ever get any better?' 'No,' she replied, 'but you get better at it!' A good response! In fact in my case I think it did 'get better' – the acute sense of loss of the first days did fade, mostly as I got on with life. For me, having a focus and a sense of purpose for my life was very important. I made the decision not to live in the past and say 'if only Roy were here' all the time. Instead I resolved to make the most of 'now': 'This is the day the Lord has made; let us rejoice and be glad in it' (Psalm 118:24). If I had one piece of advice to offer, it would be this. I knew that the longer I sat at home and grieved, the harder it would be for me to get back into things, so I resolved to get out into the world and make the most of it. There is nothing like being intimately involved with illness and death to make us value the gift of life, and to rejoice in every day when we have the strength to work and play and love and praise God.

When I became a Christian God gave me the gift of peace, and freed me from my fears: 'I am leaving you with a gift – peace of mind and heart. And the peace I give isn't fragile like the peace the world gives. So don't be troubled or afraid' (John 14:27, *Living Bible*). I did not realise it at first, but when Roy died, God added the gift of joy: 'I have told you this so that you will be filled with my joy. Yes, your cup of joy will overflow' (John 15:11, *Living Bible*). You can't manufacture joy, or pretend it; it's either there or it's not. It was only when I looked back after the first six months that I realised that even though I had been grieving, the joy was still bubbling up in me. Jesus wants our cup of joy to be full – so it's our fault if it's usually half empty!

D.L. Moody says,

There is a difference between happiness and joy. Happiness is caused by things which happen around me, and circumstances will mar it, but joy flows right on through trouble; joy flows on through the dark; joy flows in the night as well as in the day; joy flows all through persecution and opposition; it is an unceasing fountain bubbling up in the heart; a secret spring which the world cannot see and doesn't know anything about. The Lord gives his people perpetual joy when they walk in obedience to him.

It's the power of the Holy Spirit which fills us with joy, and it's the same power which enables us to persevere in times of trouble. After Roy died, there were moments when I longed to die as well, not out of any gloomy death-wish but just to be with him and be with the Lord. I wanted to take the easy way out of what I knew was going to be the uphill struggle of bereavement, and all the battles I was going to have to fight against loneliness and self-pity. Part of me was willing to work for the Lord for as long as he wanted to keep me on this earth – but oh, how much easier to go to heaven and miss out the struggle! That was when I was reminded of something Roy used to say to me when I was depressed and worn down by all the jobs I had to do: 'You will insist on thinking about everything you've got to do all at once, instead of thinking about one thing at a time!'

So I disciplined myself to take one day at a time, and trust God for the rest: 'Therefore do not worry about tomorrow, for tomorrow will worry about itself' (Matthew 6:34) – another example of putting God's word into action in our lives. Once I held on to that verse and practised it, I found that the difficulties I had built up in my mind melted away and joy took over.

That's why I didn't worry when people said that I shouldn't be cheerful, or that because I was, I couldn't have come to terms with Roy's death and the fact of my widowhood. I have faced the darkest times of my life and I have proved that 'For this I have Jesus'. I know that he will uphold and support me even through the worst problems life can offer. I feel like the man in the 'Footprints' poem, who saw two sets of footprints in the sand, one belonging to him and the other to God. He complained that at the lowest and saddest times of his life there was only one set of footprints, and said, 'I don't understand why in times when I needed you most, you would leave me.' And God replied, 'I love you and I would never leave you during your times of trials and suffering. When you see only one set of footprints, it was then that I carried you.' I certainly have had the sense of being 'carried' by God, sometimes through the prayers and love of other Christians, during the dark times of the last few years. I have discovered for myself the truth of Psalm 23:

> Even though I walk
> through the valley of the shadow of death
> I will fear no evil,
> for you are with me.

When we begin to understand this, we learn to rely on God, our only hope, the only one who is reliable and trust-worthy, the only one to whom we can turn for security and comfort. It is our daily walk with Jesus which enables us to discover the riches of God's love:

> You prepare a table before me
> in the presence of my enemies.
> You anoint my head with oil;
> my cup overflows.
> Surely goodness and mercy will follow me
> all the days of my life,
> and I will dwell in the house of the Lord
> for ever (Psalm 23:5-6).

A widower wrote: 'For months I never imagined that life would be good to me again, or that I would want it to be good. But it is, and I do. My grief has been far the deepest, most significant thing that has ever happened to me.' This strikes a chord with my experience, as I said in the inter-view I gave the day after Roy died: 'problems are growth activators'. When we face devastating circumstances we re-evaluate all our ideas about life and death, and for some, this is the first step on the way to discovering what is truly important to them in life. When we see the reality of God's power working in our lives our faith grows fast. We can never fully understand God's purposes, but sometimes when we look back we can see results – extraordinary, unimaginable results which we would never have predicted or chosen for ourselves – and we can only wonder at God's grace which can bring such fruits of love, joy and peace out of pain.

Roy's path to death led through cancer, which caused him terrible suffering. It was not the path he would have chosen, but he accepted it and said, late in his illness, 'I wouldn't have been without this experience.' We both learned such a lot about the everlasting arms of God, always beneath us and supporting us, that no price was too high to pay for that assurance. Shortly before he died, a friend told us that when praying she saw Roy 'in the palm of God's hand', and that was what it felt like – love surrounding us and holding us up.

Margaret Torrie is the founder of Cruse, the National Organisation for the Widowed. In her book *Begin Again* she says, 'The remarkable discovery we can make is that love has not deserted us, and that it is available now in a new way. Our own willingness to love and to give in the world about us is the secret of recovery and the new beginning.'[2] The part of my life that I shared with Roy has ended, and a new part has begun. I will never forget him or cease to be grateful for the wonderful years we had together, but now I have my own work to do and my own

---

[2] Margaret Torrie, *Begin Again*, Dent 1970

life to go on living. God has filled it with new friends and fresh challenges.

I have learned that for as long as we live, God has new beginnings for us, new experiences and new lessons of his love that he wants us to learn. Our path may be through 'green pastures' or through the valley of the shadow of death, but it is always the same Good Shepherd who leads us, and Jesus is with us at every stage in our journey.

> All this will be because the mercy of our God is very tender, and heaven's dawn is about to break upon us, to give light to those who sit in darkness and death's shadow, and to guide us to the path of peace (Luke 1: 78–9, *Living Bible*).

Everything that happens here on earth is but one part of an ongoing story. I know that death is something to be faced, but not feared. It is the ultimate statistic – one hundred per cent of all people die – and the only sure and predictable event of our life on earth. Yet many people spend their entire lives hiding from the very thought of it, and allow their fear of what may happen to them or their loved ones to colour their whole lives.

A friend once commented to me that many people live their life as though it were a dress rehearsal for the real thing. But in fact, by tonight we will have given the only performance of 'today' that we will ever give. So we have to put all our heart, our energy and honesty and sincerity into what we do every day. As a show business family, we found that a very suitable illustration. And every show comes to the end of its run, when we must lay aside the costumes and step off the stage, into another, larger world. For us as Christians, facing death means facing life, because we know that when we die we follow in the steps of Jesus, who himself rose from death and made possible for us a new life with a renewed and glorious body. That fact is my strength to continue as long as God chooses to keep me on this earth. I am content to accept whatever he wants for my life. So as I face tomorrow, and the next day, I place my trust in Jesus to lead me on, through love and laughter, through joy and sorrow, and through death to life everlasting.